Henry Oster

The Last Witness of Auschwitz - Life and Testimony from a Tragic Heart

Note:

....

....

....

....

....

Andrew Edward Kryzak

Book

HENRY OSTER

The Last Witness of Auschwitz - Life and Testimony from a Tragic Heart

CONTENTS

1　A GERMAN BOY

2　A NATION IN SEARCH OF A LEADER

3　JEWS IN GERMANY

4　UNDER PRESSURE

5　REPORT FOR DEPORTATION6

6　THE SOUNDS IN THE NIGHT

7　FATHERLESS CHILD

8　THE SECRET IN THE ATTIC

9　THE TRAIN

10　TO THE STABLES

11　IN THE LINE OF FIRE

12　THE GAUNTLET AND THE ONE-EYED NAZI

13　THE MARCH

14	BUCHENWALD
15	BEHIND THE WIRE AT BUCHENWALD
16	THE WELL, THE SICK AND THE DYING
17	BLACK AND WHITE
18	THE FIRST BREAKFAST
19	FEAR OF FREEDOM
20	THE LONG ROAD
21	BURYING THE DEAD
22	BOYS IN THE BARRACKS
23	ONE MORE TRAIN RIDE
24	THE RIDE BACK TO LIFE
25	WELCOME TO THE ASYLUM
26	SOMEBODY FROM SOMEWHERE
27	WHAT FREEDOM LOOKS LIKE

28	THE GOOD SHIP EXODUS
29	THE MAN FROM AMERICA
30	A FREE MAN IN PARIS
31	TO THE PROMISED LAND
32	THE WOMAN IN THE HARBOR
33	HOME AT LAST
34	WELCOME TO WESTWOOD
35	SORRY. TOO JEWISH.
36	RETURN TO GERMANY

INTRODUCTION

This book was born in Dr. Henry Oster's Beverly Hills optometrist practice. I was one of his numerous patients, and a particularly vexing one. I always found a way to grumble about my prescription as he made pair after pair of spectacles for me. If we had agreed that my right eye needed astigmatism correction at a certain angle, I would desire a slightly different twist by the time the glasses were created. Finally, in despair, he offered me a pair of old trial frames—ancient, strange-looking adjustable glasses that would allow me to shift the orientation of my lenses as much as I wanted.

I began as a patient but quickly became a friend. I was fascinated about how everything worked, and Henry, a natural teacher, was happy to explain everything to me. Appointments that would have lasted 10 minutes with another optometrist might occasionally stretch hours, with the two of us chatting while his office staff tried to keep his other patients waiting. I ended up joining him for his legendary lunches downstairs at Nibblers Restaurant on Wilshire Boulevard, where he presided over an ever-changing cast of friends and patients. Henry is 25 years my senior, yet his enthusiasm and obvious joy at being alive captivated me.

Henry seemed to regard each new day as an unexpected gift, determined to enjoy it all and persuade everyone around him to do the same. He was and still is a lot of joy to be around. I saw a faded, somewhat crooked, blue-black tattoo on his left forearm one day when he was trying, with limited success, to fit me with yet another set of contact lenses. B7648. "How did you manage to get that, Henry?" I inquired. This is how it came to be there. And how, against all odds, Henry Oster survived to tell the story after losing practically everything a human being can lose.

1

A GERMAN CHILD

I was a five-year-old German boy a long time ago. Oster, Heinz Adolf. I was a curious, lively little wise person with a shock of black hair, a double dosage of curiosity, and a restricted capacity to sit still for long periods of time.

My father was tall, solemn, trim, and well-liked. My father served in the German army, the Wehrmacht. He had fought in World War I alongside millions of other German warriors. He'd been injured in the war, with a scar on his cheek from a shrapnel strike during an artillery assault. He had received a medal for bravery. He had no excuse not to fight for his country's defense, right or wrong—to battle for his Fatherland. Like any other decent German.

The only thing that set us apart was that we were Jewish. This wasn't a big concern to me at the time. The main difference between myself and the other German youngsters I knew was that I went to synagogue with my family every Friday night instead of church on Sunday. And I attended a German Jewish school where we learned Hebrew in addition to all the other courses. But I had no idea we were any different, either better or worse than any other German family.

It was a normal, comfortable life. I was just a rambunctious German kid from a loving family living in a busy German metropolis. But when Hitler and the Nazis came to power, just as I was old enough to understand what was going on around me, everything went berserk.

My first day of school in 1934 was the first time I felt anything was wrong—my first experience of being singled out, different, and mistreated.

We were ambushed by a gang of Hitler Youth, the Deutsches Jungvolk und Jungmädel, when we came out of school that day, holding our cherished sugar cones. They were a large, boisterous horde waiting outside on the sidewalk, lads and girls our age. They were all very pleased with themselves, disguised as little Nazi Boy Scouts and Girl Scouts.

We were terrified to death. Some of my classmates were in tears. We were all young kids, about six years old. And now, after our first nerve-racking day of school, we were being attacked by a yelling Nazi mob for no apparent reason.

My parents, along with the parents of the other Jewish students, were waiting outside the school to collect us up and walk us home. However, there was little they could do to assist us. The Hitler Youth leaders pushed them all out of the way: young toughs in their teens and twenties.

When I looked up, there was a sea of uniforms and angry faces. These enraged kids in Nazi neckerchiefs, all with the identical swastika slips around their throats, were yelling and insulting us. The boys wore daggers about their waists. They were merely kids, aged ten to fourteen, but they each had their own Nazi knife. In the backdrop, we could see Nazi organizers and enthusiastic Hitler Youth parents standing with their arms crossed. They were clearly having a good time watching their youngsters show the small Jewish kids who was who and what was what.

The kids hurled rocks at us. They smacked us with sticks. We were all obliged to conduct this charade in order to escape, to reach our parents and safety. Eventually, two Cologne city police officers, who were not necessarily Nazis at the time, arrived and stopped the attack, giving me and the other Jewish kids enough time and space to reach our parents.

We were all fine—just scrapes and little cuts, with a little blood here and there. But we were all taken aback. I had gone to school that morning, full of excitement and anticipation, worried about how well I would perform in class. When I returned home that afternoon, the world had become a much darker and more deadly place. My life will never be the same after that.

2

A NATION LOOKING FOR A LEADER

It was a moment of financial struggle, a huge depression, just like in America. There was a lot of unemployment in the 1920s and early 1930s. Thousands of ragged men, many of them shell-shocked and injured combat veterans, walked the streets with nothing to do but whine, plot, and scheme.

World War I was a nightmare for its soldiers, regardless of which side they fought on. Trench warfare was terrifying, with many dying for the sake of a few yards of mud and barbed wire. Every army was plagued by disease. Millions were killed by machine guns, artillery, tanks, poison gas, and bombs dropped from airplanes and Zeppelins. The survivors, like troops today, were irrevocably changed. Millions of people were physically harmed. Almost all were hurt in their hearts and souls.

Europe would never be the same after that.

In the German economy, there was insane inflation: the same quantity of money was worth less and less every day. A loaf of bread would set you back a million marks—a wheelbarrow full of almost worthless paper money. When Hitler rose to power behind the scenes following the 1933 election, the German people were eager to follow any leader who could persuade them that he had a path out, a means to restore Germany's strength and wealth. He enlisted all those rootless, unemployed guys, ex-soldiers and veterans, and provided them with a home. He gave them a reason to fight. They now had a gang to join, something to believe in, no matter how strange and inhuman the cause turned out to be. He gathered everyone who would listen to him. He released men from prison and converted them to the Nazi cause—hardened criminals, ignorant bums, and low-life members of society. He persuaded them that they might be a part of something that would restore Germany's greatness.

He held the Jews responsible for practically all of Germany's troubles. Hitler, like many others around the world, including hero flier Charles Lindbergh and American businessman Henry Ford, felt that Jews were part of a global conspiracy.

This myth was spread by German officials in the early aftermath of World War I in order to shift blame for Germany's defeat. In 1918, Germany's allies were rapidly surrendering, and her army was running out of money, food, and reserves as it faced the increasingly powerful armies of France, the British Empire, Belgium, and the United States. Its demise was unavoidable. However, the Stab In The Back idea led many Germans, including Hitler, who was then an injured and blinded corporal in the German Army, to conclude that Germany had not been beaten, but had been weakened from within. By "others" I mean Jews and Communists.

Hitler was developing his ideology at a time when eugenics—the pseudo-science that claimed practically all human conduct was genetically influenced—was gaining appeal among white academics and authorities around the world. The eugenics movement propagated the belief that governments had the right and responsibility to prevent the "unfit" from reproducing in many countries, notably the United Kingdom and the United States.

These rules would subsequently serve as the blueprint for Nazi Germany's comparable Erbgesundheitsgericht laws, under which the Nazi regime sterilized 375,000 people, many of whom were only deaf or blind.

From 1933 through 1939, the Nazis went from sterilizing to murdering hundreds of thousands of "unfit" people. During this period, American eugenics leaders encouraged – and even financially supported – the German eugenics movement. Long before the first Jews were murdered in concentration camps, Nazi Germany's Aktion T4 program, which ran from 1939 to 1941, directed German and Austrian doctors to execute 70,273 physically or mentally disabled people through deadly medication, starvation, or poison gas.

3

IN GERMANY, THERE ARE JEWS

According to historians, the earliest Jews to settle in Germany were most likely exiles from Rome. The first documented Jewish community in Germany was established in 321 AD in Cologne. Which is also my hometown. So, by the time Adolf Hitler (who was born in Austria, not Germany) and his Nazi colleagues determined that Jews like me, my mother, and my father were unworthy to reside in "his" Germany, we had already been there for almost 1,600 years.

Pogroms, or waves of persecution, raged on and off for hundreds of years. Jews were occasionally attacked, separated, and ridiculed. When the pendulum swung back, we were more welcomed within European society. For nearly a thousand years, Jews had been persecuted as easy scapegoats in Europe and worldwide. During the First Crusade, which began in 1096, Christians in Germany were encouraged to attack and murder non-believers. Entire Jewish communities throughout Germany were massacred. Muslims, who were no more popular than Jews, were in the Holy Land, a great way away. But we Jews were right in town, waiting to be killed.

During the fourteenth century, the Jews were blamed for the rat-borne epidemic known as the Black Death, which killed up to half of the residents of many major cities in central Europe. Rumors spread that the cause was Jews poisoning the wells of Christians, inciting the terrified people to lash out in horrifying ways against Jewish communities.

Because Jews were frequently segregated in city ghettos, restricting the spread of the plague, and because Jews at the period observed usually greater hygiene standards than other civilizations, Jewish communities often suffered significantly fewer cases of the epidemic. This arouses suspicion among the Catholics and other residents, who retaliate in many cases by massacring Jewish communities, frequently destroying entire populations of Jews, as well as their homes and synagogues.

Cologne's Jewish community was annihilated in 1349. Men, women, and children were tortured, beheaded, and burned alive, and their homes and belongings were seized. Just two years later, in 1351, as many as 60 large German Jewish settlements, as well as 150 smaller villages, had been annihilated.

In other situations, Jewish communities chose to burn down their own homes while their families remained inside to avoid crowds from dragging them out and burning or lynching them. As a result of these atrocities, the Holy Roman Emperor, Charles IV, declared Jewish property forfeit, providing local authorities with even less incentive to prevent the wholesale elimination of the Jewish people.

After all, Jesus of Nazareth was a Jew who was persecuted and murdered by the Romans. Finally, in the 1860s, German Jews and other non-Christian Germans were granted full legal rights under German law. When the North German Confederation was created in 1869, Jews were granted the same rights as any other German citizen after nearly 1,500 years of separation and suppression.

4

UNDER STRESS

At the Nazi Party rally in Nuremberg in 1935, a wide set of regulations was passed that codified many of the anti-Jewish measures that were wreaking havoc on our lives. The Nazis forced us to hand over all of our belongings, including anything of worth. Jews were not permitted to own a home, a car, or even a newspaper or magazine subscription. We couldn't ride the streetcars, go to the movies, or sit on park seats. Signs reading "Juden Verboten"—"No Jews Allowed"—appeared throughout the city. Worst of all, Jews were not permitted to operate their own enterprises, many of which they had created from the bottom up and passed down through the generations.

It was still possible for some people to find a way out of Germany until 1938. Some of our family and friends were able to get out of this chaos and flee to another nation. The method of escaping was quite challenging. You required permission to leave Germany at the time because it was a police state. This means that the government has access to every citizen's personal information. You couldn't travel on vacation until you registered with the new police department where you went. You had to register in the new location if you were gone for seven days. When you return home, you must re-register. The paperwork was ridiculous, straight out of Franz Kafka.

The irony is that the original Nazi/German concept was to eliminate Jews in whatever way possible. At first, a large number of Jews were permitted to emigrate. Some others fled to Palestine, which is now known as Israel. Some made it across the mountains into Switzerland. Some carried special passports with a large "J" for Jude—German for Jew. You could leave Germany with one of those passports, but you couldn't return.

Another issue was that in order to leave Germany, you needed to find a country willing to accept you. And none of the main Western countries, including the United States, were willing to take in the tens of thousands, if not hundreds of thousands, of Jews who found themselves suddenly without property, money, or jobs, which Germany did not want. Only a few countries accepted a small number of Jewish refugees. In South America, Paraguay and Uruguay enabled a few families to purchase their way in. And, thanks to the activities of some heroic Japanese and Chinese officials, around 20,000 Jews were allowed to remain in a confined ghetto in Japanese-occupied Shanghai, China.

5

DEPORTATION REPORT

One day, in October of 1941, when I was twelve, a Gestapo courier came to the apartment with an official notice. We were to report for "resettlement." We were puzzled and bewildered. Crammed into our closet-like apartment room, we kept asking each other questions that none of us could begin to answer. We were resigned to reporting on Monday morning, but late on Saturday night, the soldiers came to our crowded apartment again. They had apparently decided that if we were going to run, to attempt to avoid our deportation on Monday, they were most likely to catch us, unprepared, a couple nights before. We had no food, and the Germans didn't give us any—all they gave us was water. Some people had smuggled some candy into their suitcases, and that night it was like gold, some of the luckier people feeding the kids, like me, whatever they had.

The next day we were loaded onto a small train, with just a few passenger cars. We were locked inside, with no way to escape. The train rocked and screeched east across Germany. The conditions were awful. We rotated so everybody could sit some of the time and then take a turn standing. There were not enough toilets for all these people, so very soon the cars smelled like latrines. There were children crying. Babies screaming. Shocked mothers and fathers trying to reassure their kids that everything was going to be alright, even though we were sure that it was going to be anything but all right.

Finally, we pulled into a dirty, unkempt city. The people on the streets looked even more miserable than we felt. They were unshaven, clothed in tattered rags. They looked starved, beaten and exhausted.

"Where are we?" asked a man from the train, as we pulled into the station.

"You're in Poland, in the city of Łódź," said a walking skeleton on the platform. "Welcome to the ghetto."

Even before the war, Poland was a severely impoverished country in comparison to Germany, with widespread poverty. The Germans crammed us into crude apartment dwellings that were nothing more than brick constructions with rooms. There were no toilets, running water, gas, heat, or furniture. Some of the windows were shattered, exposing us to the harsh Polish winter in the middle of October—it was so cold that if you spat, your saliva would freeze before it struck the ground. The ghetto cops crammed 21 people, including my father, mother, and me, into a room no bigger than a child's bedroom.

The ghetto as a whole housed 160,000 people. These were crammed into only 20,000 rooms, many of which were uninhabitable due to cracked floors and disintegrating walls. It was as if a tornado had ripped through the city.

6

THE SOUNDS AT NIGHT

My father and mother were granted their work assignments within a few days. My parents were keen to acquire employment because the ghetto police had told us that if we worked, we would get extra food rations. My mother was compelled to work in a factory that produced Stiefel Platten, which are small iron toe and heel plates for German jackboot bottoms that extend the life of the leather. My father was assigned to repair the ghetto fence, including the posts, barbed wire, and electric wire that had been smashed through or had fallen into disrepair.

My father had saved a letter from the Kaiser detailing his military duty and the medals he had acquired, which kept us from going straight to an extermination camp like Chelmno or Treblinka. I later realized that letter rescued us from certain death.

Working in the farm field did provide some relief for me. It was hard, but at least I was outdoors, away from all the people and the noise and the stench, doing something useful.

We were miserable, but because we had only been there a short time, we were in better shape than those who had been before us. People in the ghetto aged quickly. Because of the lack of food, the backbreaking work, and the disease that raced through the communities, your life expectancy was roughly six months. Consider 21 individuals sleeping in a small room all night. If one person became ill, everyone became ill.

The ód ghetto was effectively a death chamber. The Germans had decided that nearly everyone sent to ód at the time would be murdered in one of the massive extermination camps: Chelmno, Treblinka, or Auschwitz.

There was only so much space in the camps. Capacity to live—or capacity to kill and dispose of bodies. So, ód and the other ghettos were storage areas for the Nazis, a place to keep the Jews of Europe until it was our turn to die.

The Nazis would try to get as much work out of us as possible, wherever we were, since they needed slave labor to create food, uniforms, and war supplies of all kinds, from boots to bullets to bombers. They had carefully evaluated how long it was worth it to keep a prisoner alive. A Jew could be useful to the war effort for a few months, even under harsh, near-starvation conditions. When a group had lived in the ghetto for a long enough period of time and had become too weak, malnourished, or depleted, they would round them up and ship them away. The slaves would thereafter be replaced by new arrivals—Jews from the seized nations, presumably in better health.

Just like we had replaced the tired, despondent Jews who had come before us.

7

ABANDONED CHILD

My father's job was difficult and risky since he had to maintain the ghetto fence. The Germans stationed guard towers along the border, ready to fire at anything that moved. They were liable to shoot if you got too close to the fence, even if it was your job to fix it.

My father's wound appeared to be minor—a graze across the fleshy part of his arm. He'd been wounded before, during World War I, so he toughed it out—he pretended it wasn't a big issue. My mother cleaned and dressed the wound, and my father returned to work the next day. He didn't have a choice. He didn't get any meals if he didn't work. And we were already on the verge of hunger. He arrived home from work early about a month later. He had felt considerably weaker than usual, so he had been allowed to leave work an hour or two earlier than usual. I recall his saying, "I'm so tired," when he walked in.

He was so weak the day he got home early that he had difficulty getting up to our room. "God, I could hardly make it up the stairs, I'm so tired," he moaned. I was standing near a sleeping spot on the floor—we didn't have a bed, so he had to sleep on the floor, on a blanket we shared with the other guests. I had no clue he was that sick. I was there with my mother and two other women, family friends, to keep an eye on him. "Hans, Hans!" shouted my mum. And he didn't say anything. He simply stared at the ceiling, his eyes wide open. Deep in his throat, he gurgled.

My mother saw he wasn't breathing. "Er ist weg," she muttered as softly as she could. "He is gone." It was calm, simple, and uncomplicated. He simply wasn't there any longer.

Many years later, in the books from the Łód ghetto hospital, I discovered the official German documentation of my father's death. Which is hilarious given that he never went to the hospital; he simply came home one day, lay down on his blanket, and died. His death was attributed to "bronchial catarrh" or pneumonia. I don't recall any doctors or other medical personnel visiting the house, but it's possible that after he died, the local ghetto officials arrived and obtained information about how he died from my mother or someone else in the room.

8

THE KEY TO THE ATTIC

The Germans came for us one hot, muggy night in July 1943. It was a raid, as we had heard in other parts of the ghetto. We, like so many others before us, had been chosen to vanish.

A trap door opened to a small attic chamber just above the door, above the transom. I pushed the trap door open by stepping on the door handle and raising myself up on the edge of the transom. I could reach down and grab my mother's hands once I was up there, and pull her up with me. I was frail, but she weighed next to nothing at the time.

After a few days, a fresh group of Jews walked into our room, looking just as plump and healthy as we did six months previously. We were again crammed in, elbow to elbow. After a few months, another nocturnal raid occurred. I did the same thing, sheltering my mother and myself in the attic behind a thick rafter. I felt bad for not telling the others where we were hiding. But if I had told them, we'd all been captured. Even after all these years, I still feel wrong about it. I know I did it to help my mum and myself.

9

THE RAILWAY

We were herded out of the courtyard and onto a narrow street by the Germans. We didn't have to walk far. There was a railroad siding nearby, a strongly guarded station where people and materials were carried in and out of ód—the location where we had entered the ghetto months previously.

Six closed, rugged boxcars were waiting for us. There could have been a couple hundred individuals crammed inside each rough wooden box with us. The train began to chugg and rattle along. The roofs were scorched by the scorching August sun. And the heat of so many people crammed into such a small place began to take its toll.

I turned and came to a halt to assist my mum. She was exhausted and starved, and she was really thin. She was 43 years old that night, but she appeared elderly, frail, and fragile, almost like a skeleton.

I attempted to hold on to her and assist her in any way I could. We pulled her to the ground with the help of a handful of other men, our feet sliding and unsteady on the sharp gravel close to the long concrete railway station.

There were a lot of soldiers, officers, and SS shoving us around. They roared and smacked into the swaying flood of children, women, and men. "Men to the right," they exclaimed. "Women, move to the left!"

For a split second, I knew they were separating my mother and me. They were tearing into us. It seemed as if we were grabbed in a cyclone and dragged away from each other into the sky. It had a force to it, a whoosh that I could feel.

Her eyes were filled with puzzlement, horror, and perplexity. She was probably seeing the same thing in me. I was fifteen years old, a young guy, her son. I was attempting to look after her. She was my mother, and she was attempting to look after me. And neither of us was able to do anything.

We had little time to say our final goodbyes. We were yanked apart, and that was the end of it. It seemed like someone had yanked my arm off. She'd been dragged into the queue with the other women.

10

GOING TO THE STABLES

I remembered my mum being taken away from me the night we arrived. That first night in Auschwitz, I knew she'd gone to the gas chambers and subsequently the ovens. I remembered being cold beneath my matted uniform. That I was exhausted, thirsty, hungry, and caked in dirt, sweat, and my own filth. That my bones burned from tossing and turning on a rough-hewn wooden rack with five other men. And I realized that if I didn't get my frail body into the courtyard quickly enough, I'd be dragged into the next of these dark, bleak mornings.

If a prisoner fell out of ranks, fainted, or attracted attention in any way, the guards beat him with their pistols, swagger sticks, or steel-toed boots. If the prisoner died as a result of the beating, so be it—the corpse was already in line, in place, and ready to be counted.

We young recruits, 131 in total, were separated from the rest and commanded to form four-by-four columns. After a half-hour march through barbed-wire gates, fields, and past administration buildings, we arrived at another group of low wooden buildings that appeared to be painted replicas of the wooden barracks we had left behind in Birkenau.

The SS officials broke us into groups of 10 or twelve and assigned us to one of the barracks. When we approached the facilities, expecting to see rows of sleeping shelves, we were instead greeted by rows of stalls filled with snorting, sighing, painting horses.

The stable housed twenty-eight horses, the majority of whom were pregnant mares set to offer their offspring to the German war effort.

Europe, particularly Eastern Europe, remained predominantly a horse-drawn civilization, and the Germans required every drop of gasoline for their tanks, vehicles, and Luftwaffe jets. It was also discovered that the railroad gauge—the spacing between the rails—was wider in Russia than in Germany, rendering the German engines and cars worthless until the tracks were modified. As a result, the Germans needed hundreds of thousands of draft horses to transport personnel, weapons, and supplies throughout the conquered countries, and this stable complex was just one of hundreds constructed to meet that demand.

Each of us boys was given three or four mares to look after. The Germans made it abundantly clear that the horses were far more valuable than the prisoners: if something happened to one of the horses in our care, or to its foal, we could be certain that we would not be assigned another; we would become the "Sunday Entertainment," just as in the ód ghetto—we would be hung at the main gate, at high noon, with the camp's military band providing a grim soundtrack.

Our work at the stables rapidly became normal. After the pre-dawn roll-call in front of our barracks in the main camp, we marched about a mile out to the stables in two lines. After a twelve- to sixteen-hour labor, we would be marched back in the evening, always after dark. When we—the 130 stable boys and I—were sent to the Auschwitz stables, I was given two horses to care for: two mares that were already pregnant with that season's foals. I was supposed to learn how to assist the mares during mating, monitor them throughout their pregnancies, and ensure they gave birth without incident.

We learned that if we fed the horses every day, we could sneak a little bit of food every now and then. When the Germans weren't watching, we could hide a few oats or carrots. We may also steal milk from mares after they give birth. Sometimes the foals would get sick shortly after birth: they would suffer diarrhea and lose the desire to suckle from their moms. We would also give the foals water instead of mare's milk in secret, so the mares would have milk left over. When that happened, we were able to take a few mouthfuls of horse milk when the guards weren't looking.

It would have all been over if the military had caught us. They held inspections every day, forcing us to open our lips so they could examine inside with a torch. You were done if they discovered some chewed carrot fragments or an oat pocket. Simply put, you'd be taken away and hanged the following Sunday. When we did eat something during the day, we made sure to immediately wash our mouths to cover the evidence.

It's amazing what you can accomplish when your life's on the line. It was worth risking your life because if you didn't eat enough—which we never did—you'd starve in a few weeks anyhow.

11

IN THE LINE OF DUTY

In all the years since I was imprisoned in Auschwitz, there is one story I have never told anyone, one event I have never shared. It was a Saturday evening. We were returning to the camp from the stables, and I was at the tail end of the line of convicts. Because of the extra labor with the stallion, I was the last lad to finish and lock the barn before we marched back to the main camp in our normal rows of four across. As we fumbled through the darkness, I observed something weird going on at the main gate. We ended up against the wall in the middle of the night, not knowing if we were going to live or die. I recall it being quite cold. We had no idea what was about to occur. But we knew it wasn't going to go well.

A rustle of cloth was heard, followed by a gasp and cry from the inmates. When I looked up, the back canvas curtains of the trucks at the front of the courtyard had been abruptly yanked up. Two machine-gun crews concealed in the vehicles began to fire, their muzzles gleaming in the darkness, spraying bullets directly into the gathering of detainees. Directly at me. When we heard machine-gun fire, our immediate response was to go down, away from the sound, to duck and try to avoid the explosions and bullets. We were at the back because we were the last group to be chosen. I had a really tall guy in front of me who was injured by the first gunshot.

He pushed back on top of me, and I felt a pain in my knee before collapsing beneath a heap of flailing, heaving, dying men. When the shooting began, there were so many people packed in so tightly that the gunmen didn't have a clear shot at the victims in the rear. We were also small, mere youngsters in comparison to the other soldiers, so the machine gunners had been forced to shoot down at us from the truck bed's height, and had missed some of us in the commotion.

The machine-gun fire halted, but wounded prisoners were screaming and wailing and scrambling on the ground, away from the bullets, attempting to do all they could to survive. I could see two German officers, with their pistols drawn, rummaging among the pile of dead and dying men as I peered over the shoulder of the body ahead of me. They were firing the injured laying defenseless on the ground in the backs of their heads one by one.

My stablemates had likewise survived the first volley of gunshots. We were trapped in a little pocket in the back, surrounded by the dead and dying, where the bullets had missed us. There was a door not far away, a door to the next building on the courtyard's edge. I knew it would lead to a corridor that ran the length of the building. I suggested to my buddies that we all sprint together to see if we could make it to the door in time. They would have had a clear shot at each of us if we had gone one by one, but if we all went together—and remember, we were very small—we might have a chance. We were surrounded by blood, body parts, and death. It was our only opportunity.

I wasn't really hurt. It seemed more like a graze wound than a bullet hole. I was able to conceal it from the block elder and the other boys. When I was alone, I made sure to remove the blood and feces from my clothing and fix the hole in my pants leg so the Germans wouldn't notice and think I was one of the inmates who had escaped the massacre.

I got away with it in the midst of all the chaos, among all those thousands of convicts. They would have found me out if I had been hit a little worse, if I had failed to show up to work the next day, or the day after that.

What do you do if you don't have bandages, a doctor, or drugs to treat a gunshot wound? You urinate on it to sterilize it as much as possible. You cover it with snot if it becomes infected. You extract it directly from your nose, which is continually flowing in the cold, and utilize it as a protective film as well as a type of antibiotic.

If I wasn't scared before, I am terrified now. I was broken to remember what we had been through, to know that we had been chosen to die, that we had been machine shot, and that we had survived for no apparent reason. The other stable guys in my group who had been chosen to be shot likewise made it out of the courtyard and returned to the barracks. Perhaps the German gunners were hesitant to fire at boys rather than men. Perhaps they missed us because we were small and difficult to see in the dark, at the back of the condemned crowd.

12

THE NAZI WITH ONE EYE AND THE GAUNTLET

I was quickly hired as a runner for the stables. Every day, just like in the Łódź ghetto, I had to deliver the reports back to the administrative office. Because I only had three horses to look after, the Germans decided I had the time for an extra chore, and because I spoke German, I was likely to have less trouble getting through the camp: if a German challenged me or wanted to know what I was doing, I could tell him in his own language, giving me some leeway to move around between the stables and the administrative buildings.

My employment as a runner offered me some flexibility to find food, but it also put me in situations that terrified me. In Auschwitz, you could mislead yourself into thinking you were relatively safe one minute and then be dead the next. So I had no idea what I was getting myself into.

We were given showers every twenty days or so in a special barrack block near to the camp's main toilet. We stable lads were marched in after work, long after dark, and told to remove our clothes. The Nazis were always on the lookout for signals of weakness. There were continually new arrivals at Auschwitz. People who were already there had to die to make room. This was the last in the series. If you appeared to be in pain, sick, or starving, you would be chosen for execution.

The trucks were still out there, and I could hear the crying from within the building. I tried to stay inside as long as possible. I had no intention of going back out if I didn't have to—I was hoping the trucks would move ahead on their dreadful voyage so I wouldn't be forced into one of them. I knew my sheaf of documents had saved me coming in because they gave me an air of purpose and authority, but if I walked back through that corridor of death without the papers, it would look like I was fleeing. That's exactly what an escapee would do.

The maimed officer saw that I was lingering for a longer period of time than normal. "Get out of here," he demanded. I pointed to the crowd situation near the gate. "How do I know the guards will not shoot me when I walk through?" I questioned, my voice quivering. With one eye, he gazed out the window. "I see." He got to his feet and proceeded for the entrance. "You don't need to worry," he said. "I'll walk out there with you."

Walking through the iron gate and up that graveyard of a road, we must have looked like an odd couple—a ghost-pale Jewish adolescent and a mutilated SS officer. He walked with me past the trucks, then turned around and followed me up the road. I was so terrified that I peed myself. I had to hang my clothes up to dry when I got back to the stables.

13

THE MOVE

We were gathered in the Play Appellplatz one day near the end of January—January 23, 1945, to be exact. The SS informed us that we would be marched to another camp in the west. We gathered our limited belongings, in my case just my clothes and a battered cup that was still dangling from the soiled rope around my neck. A handful of the prisoners were able to carry an old blanket draped around their necks, or even a small mattress slung over their shoulders, as we left the barracks behind. We were organized into a larger group of roughly a thousand persons by the SS. We started walking in the bitter cold Polish winter, without food or water. We were led down a paved road that was slick with snow, ice, and slush, with agriculture on one side and forest on the other. The long road ahead of us vanished into the distance. Everywhere, as if hurled by some reckless, massive hand. Like everyone else in that macabre parade, I just kept dragging along, going as slowly as I could to conserve energy while keeping up with the ones ahead of me. And never, ever stop, slow down, or stand out in any manner. We finally dragged ourselves to a train side in the late afternoon. The Germans squeezed us as closely as tattered human bodies can be jammed into open-topped freight carriages.

The train had four carriages, each with about 200 or 250 people crowded inside. We weren't as cold now, and being crammed in with everyone else gave us a sense of security. I have no idea how much time went on the train. I was fatigued, numb, and practically unconscious as a result of hunger and thirst. I slipped in and out of sleep, nodding along with the cars' swaying and clattering on the tracks. I was awakened by a terrible boom and throb pouring down from the heavens. I'd seen German planes with the cross and swastika, but these speeding, olive-drab planes had large, circular red-and-white emblems on their wings and fuselages. I've learned that these were British fighter-bombers, most likely Hawker

Typhoons. The jets flew over us and then vanished over the horizon. They returned to attack mode, strafing the train with their roaring 20 mm cannons. Hundreds of bursting rounds ripped into the cars and their occupants.

I was one of the first few detainees to be crammed into my car. So I was pushed up into the right front corner, partially shielded by the car's front wall. The captives in the back of our car were not so fortunate. A 20mm cannon shell is about the size of your thumb and travels twice as fast as sound. When the shells impacted, they detonated, tearing people apart. Because we were crammed in so tightly, a single shell could kill a large number of captives. A boy would arrive for a split second, then vanish in a blaze of blood, bone, cloth, and flesh. All of this was taking place just a few feet away from me.

A walking rain of bullets killed the German machine gunner situated on the back wall of my automobile. He sagged over his gun like a rag doll, his helmet clattering down on the captives, blood streaming from his head. The jets must have run out of fuel or ammunition because they were coming at us one minute and then the noise stopped and the train continued to move. The devastation in the back of our automobile was terrifying. It appeared that a bomb had gone off at a butcher store. Several captives had been killed, and scores more were writhing and crying, dying of horrific wounds or simply bleeding to death. The train kept moving, blood pouring from the cars and onto the rails. We might have all been killed by the planes if the train had stopped or been crippled.

14

BUCHENWALD

The train's wheels shrieking on the iron rails jolted me awake. I'd been curled up in the same position for hours and didn't know whether I'd ever be able to straighten up again.Outside, the German guards wrenched the rusted doors open, and the survivors of the voyage began to pour out, some landing on their feet, others simply collapsing to the gray gravel railroad yard. When the fresh air reached my corner, I crawled, then rolled across the blood-, urine-, and vomit-covered wooden floor toward the door.I attempted to cushion my fall by hanging my legs over the side of the door, but my legs simply refused to unfold. I couldn't stand up after two other inmates grabbed my shoulders and threw me to the ground.

When we arrived, only about 400 people remained alive."Welcome to Buchenwald," one of the inmates unloading the train stated.I had some unusual ties to Buchenwald. Unlike the previous horrible places I'd been taken to, I knew something about it. I remembered my cousin Walter telling me everything about it back in 1939, when we were all jammed into a little apartment in Cologne. Before Walter left the apartment and attempted to flee Germany by climbing over the Alps into Switzerland, he told us about being imprisoned at Buchenwald after being apprehended on November 9, the legendary Night of Broken Glass—Kristallnacht. He was among the 30,000 Jewish men who had been apprehended that night—the round-up from which my father had escaped thanks to his friendship with the hotel doorman. Walter's apartment had been set on fire by the Nazis, so he leaped out the window to escape. However, he was apprehended. He was a prisoner at Buchenwald the next thing he knew.Walter was obliged to work as a slave to extend the camp, to build it up and prepare it for all the convicts who were going to arrive.He informed us about the crimes he observed in Buchenwald, how inhumane the conditions were, and how vicious the Germans were. I'd been at Buchenwald for about two months, through

February and March, when the food and water ran out. It was as if the Germans, who had been so intent on imprisoning and exterminating us all, had simply forgotten that we were still alive.

There was a sensation of dread. A sensation of impending disaster. When the food ran out, people began to perish all around us. When someone died, the Germans did not even remove the body. The bodies were left in their bunks for days at a time. We convicts lacked the strength to move them, and the Germans wouldn't let us. As a result, the barracks were transformed into strange mausoleums, with the living lying alongside the dead. To keep the dead bodies from entirely decaying, the damned Germans threw chlorine powder on them. Because of the stifling chlorine fumes, those of us who were still alive were compelled to cram into the upper bunks, away from the stink and sickness. We were entirely shut in at night. The troops would shoot if we went outside to take a few deep breaths.

This continued for eleven days. There is no food. There is almost no water. I lost what little strength I had after a few days. My stomach had shrunk so drastically, into a knot, that I couldn't even stand up straight. I was a sixteen-year-old boy curled in a ball on a hard wooden bunk, looking like an emaciated one-hundred-year-old man. There was absolutely no sanitation. The rotting bodies and filth from those of us who were still alive made it impossible to survive in the barracks. Flies, maggots, and lice were drawn to the bodies. But we couldn't do anything but wait.

15

BUCHENWALD BEHIND THE WIRE

The Russians and other Communist prisoners had taken control of their part of Buchenwald in the days before the Americans arrived. They had buried covert weapon caches in various locations across the camp. There had been a tense standoff between the Communists, who ran the camp inside the barbed wire, and the SS and SS Oberführer Hermann Pister, the camp commandant, who was a weak man, prone to delaying decisions, and who realized that the American military advance across Germany made Buchenwald's liberation a matter of time.

The Communists were aware that Heinrich Himmler, the Nazi commander of the SS, had ordered the execution of all detainees and the destruction of the camps. However, the Communist detainees had very strong intelligence on what was going on outside, and they did everything they could to slow down the SS and keep as many Jews and other camp inmates safe as possible—especially us children.

The camp inmate commanders recognized that even with their arsenal of weaponry, they would be no match for the 3,000 or so SS guards if an all-out uprising broke out. They hoped that by refusing to assemble as commanded by the Nazis, they could slow down the Nazi death machine until the Allies arrived and liberated the camp. They had even built a radio transmitter and were sending out urgent SOS calls, urging the Americans to arrive as quickly as possible.

Despite this, many Jews were slain in the last several days. We heard through the camp grapevine that the Nazis would occasionally order groups of Jews and others to report to the Appellplatz, where they would be dragged away to death marches or shot in the woods. Just four days before the liberation, on April 7, a train loaded with Jews marched out of Buchenwald and was taken east, toward the Dachau concentration camp near Munich. On April 27, the train finally arrived. During that period, many of the Jews on board had died from starvation, illness, or being strafed by Allied fighter planes, just as my train had been a few months before.

The Nazis attempted to gather forty-six of the most active prisoner leaders, tipped off by a turncoat within the camp, to be taken away and shot at one point. However, thanks to their excellent spy network within the camp, the inmate underground was able to hide almost all of those on the list—underneath barracks or in other secret places, or exchange their identities with prisoners who had already died—making it nearly impossible for the SS to tell who was who and who to shoot. Another time during those final days, word came that the few English and American detainees in the camp would be executed. They were secreted in tunnels and sunken hiding places beneath barracks across the camp, and were supplied with food and water whenever the Nazis turned their backs.

My fellow teenagers and I, as young Jews who had only lately arrived in Buchenwald, were not a part of any of this. We were isolated in the Little Camp, the most dangerous and heavily guarded area of the camp, and had no idea what was going on.

The convict leaders were unsure whether they could rely on any of us. When individuals are as desperate to survive as we were, they will do anything, including spy on their fellow inmates, for a slice of food. We were new and inexperienced, and by that point, we were in such bad form that we wouldn't have been much good in a fight. We did everything we could in my section of the camp to keep our heads down. To pretend to be non-existent—a talent I had honed in Auschwitz for years.

A few days before the camp was liberated, the Germans started to realize that lingering near Buchenwald would be bad for their health. They abandoned their stations and attempted to flee, some of them removing their SS uniforms and dressing in civilian clothes to avoid the Allied soldiers and the camp's vengeful prisoners.

On the day of liberation, some Russian POWs pursued the escaping SS guards north into the forests and fields, and south toward the city of Weimar. Many of the SS men did not survive. The Russians were determined to exact their vengeance. The Germans had been particularly ruthless on the Eastern Front, and these Russians were not about to let them off the hook.

Many of the SS guards were apprehended, beaten, and kicked to death by Russians or German Communists who were also imprisoned. We later learned that some of the guards were lynched by vengeful convicts. They'd been hung from trees near where they'd been apprehended.

The first Americans to enter Buchenwald did so by chance. The crew of a Third Army armored car, which resembled a miniature tank on wheels and was commanded by Captain Frederic Keffer, had been tasked with scouting the fields and forest north of Weimar. They noticed a group of SS guards fleeing the camp, followed by a swarm of fugitive Russian convicts attempting to apprehend and murder them. The Russians informed the American scouting unit of the location of the camp, and a couple of the Russians got into the armored car to serve as guides past the barbed wire and into the camp.

Captain Keffer and his assistant, Jewish American G.I. Technical Sergeant Herbert Gottshalk, left their armored car outside the camp with two other G.I.s and stepped into the property through a hole in the barbed wire on the north side of the enclosure. They were met with a scene of complete anarchy, with thousands of convicts celebrating their release. According to Captain Keffer's report, several of the stronger convicts repeatedly took the Americans by their arms and legs and flung them into the air in joy. Captain Keffer was flung around so forcefully that he became dizzy and had to order the inmates to stop their wild liberation demonstration.

My barrack was nowhere near where these first two entered the camp, so we didn't find out until a little later, when a small squadron of US tanks ran over the barbed wire on the south and roared into the camp.

16

THE WELL, THE ILL, AND THE DIETING

I was lying on the ground in front of our barracks, trying to grasp the fact that it was all over. I was curled up in a ball, crippled by weakness and stomach aches caused by malnutrition. But I was still alive. The scene was surreal. Some of the inmates were hallucinating. Screaming, crying, and shouting could be heard everywhere.

As more Americans arrived, they drove up the slope in their jeeps and trucks. They hadn't come prepared to save tens of thousands of starving skeletons, so they offered us whatever food they could find. I recall one GI giving me a stick of chewing gum. I had no idea what chewing gum was, so I kept trying to eat it, but it wouldn't dissolve. I had no idea what to do with it, so I just swallowed it whole.

Another soldier handed me a tin of pork, which I assumed was Spam. It was the most delicious thing I had ever tasted. As the afternoon moved towards nightfall, the Americans became increasingly organized. Medics arrived and began the triage process, dividing the detainees into three groups.

The first group consisted of the healthiest males, those who did not require immediate medical assistance. The second group was made up of men and boys who severely required assistance—food, drink, and medical attention—but who were likely to live.

The dying were the third group. Even though they were alive and free, it did not guarantee that they would live to see the next day. It was the medics' dreadful task to pick who they could and could not save.

That first night, there were few supplies and only a few workers to care for the worst patients. Many boys and men perished before they could be saved by food, clean water, and medicine. My friend Ivar, who could hardly stand, was chosen to be treated. He was what the Germans in the camps called a musselman—Yiddish for Muslim—at the time, their harsh, prejudiced way of declaring he was too far gone to salvage. However, the Americans disagreed and chose him to be treated, most likely due to his size and age.

Once we were separated from the rest of the detainees due to our medical conditions, American medics and soldiers separated us lads from the rest of the inmates. It made sense: the Americans were directly accountable for us youngsters, but the adults were free to come and leave, at least technically. I also wondered if we were kept alive for the same reason the Germans wanted to kill as many young Jews as they could: because we represented the next generation of an entire people.

An officer led us out of the barbed-wire prisoner compound and went to the stone buildings where the German SS guards had been housed. The place was filthy and run-down, yet it had actual heat and light, and it appeared to us to be a palace. Most of the youngsters, including myself, had their own personal bunk bed to sleep on.

German SS officers slept on twin bunks, while enlisted soldiers slept in three-high bunks. I had the good fortune to end myself in an officers' block, in one of the double bunks. This would be the first mattress I'd slept on since we were evicted from our Cologne flat in 1935. Sleeping on bare wood for ten years. Of course, we were all really hungry. As we gained strength, we gained the guts to complain to our hosts, these overfed Americans who were racing around attempting to keep order.

They declined to offer us much food that first evening, fearing that an uncontrolled intake of food might overload our famished digestive systems and cause more harm than good. This seemed absurd to us.

We were hungry and in desperate need of nourishment. Every cell in my body was screaming for bread, meat, potatoes, cheese, and whatever else I could get my hands on. But the medics replied no calmly and firmly. They told us we'd be given little quantities, a bit more each day, to prevent us from dying from the shock of eating too much, too fast.

I'm thankful they did. Those prisoners who didn't have such guidance suffered: the adult men who were liberated that day were completely free, though the Americans tried to keep all the prisoners corralled in the camp to avoid interfering with the war effort and to prevent some overeager American machine gunner or fighter pilot from mistaking them for German troops and shooting them. Some of these detainees were Russian POWs, or prisoners of war. They were confined in a separate subcamp, separated from us by barbed wire. These individuals were generally in better shape than we were. The Nazis had treated them with some decency, at least during my time in Buchenwald. But, like us, they had been famished for the previous ten days or so.

By the time the Americans arrived, or shortly thereafter, many of the Russians, German Communists, and political detainees had already departed the camp. They were adults, and our allies in the United States military had no official say in where they went or what they did. They were scurrying over the countryside, gathering food wherever they could, primarily in the form of livestock "liberated" from nearby farms. They hauled sheep, cows, pigs, and chickens back to camp, butchered them, and then prepared a massive supper in the massive camp kitchen. They ate like pigs, which was exactly what each of us desired.

The outcome was terrifying. Hundreds of them were overwhelmed by the greasy food's assault on their systems. Their stomachs, like mine, had shrunk to the point that they couldn't process anything. If you don't eat for an extended period of time, a flood of food might simply block up and overwhelm the system, driving you into shock and, in many cases, death. That is exactly what happened to many of those unfortunate, voracious Russians and other elderly detainees. They collapsed and died horrific, agonizing deaths, victims of their own primal hunger. On the day they were rescued, their bodies lay in the Appellplatz, some of them alive, many of them not.

Evening rapidly turned to darkness in our own repurposed SS barrack. As the lights came on, the healthier kids began to act like teenage boys again, talking back and forth. As the thrill of our escape wore off, I was overtaken with exhaustion and weakness and fell asleep.

For the first time in what felt like an eternity, I could sleep knowing that I would be free in the morning.

17

WHITE AND BLACK

When I awoke the morning after our escape, it took me a few moments to grasp that this was not just another dream, one from which I would soon awaken, thrown back into the nightmare that had been my existence for so many years. It was true that I was lying alone on a warm, soft mattress. The clamor around me, of youngsters waking up and climbing out of their mattresses, jolted me awake. There was one item lacking. There were no Germans yelling. Nobody told me what to do, which was a strange sensation. It was as if I had gone deaf in the middle of the night.

I was still really weak and hungry. But, like everyone else, I staggered outside onto the Appellplatz for the morning roll-call. This was unlike any other roll-call we had ever experienced. For the first time, after all those gloomy, bleak mornings and years of living in continuous fear of being beaten or worse, every second of every day, we were lining up of our own free choice. The American physicians and soldiers faced the daunting task of feeding and protecting all 21,000 rescued prisoners at Buchenwald. So there was a lot going on right in front of our befuddled, skeleton faces.

After being brutalized for years by German SS, German criminals, and other Eastern European guards, it was difficult to trust these new warriors at first. The Americans appeared weird to us, as if they had dropped from another planet. And I'm sure we appeared equally strange to them. After what we'd been through, most of us didn't appear human. We were filthy, starving, dressed in rags or nothing, and spoke a hodgepodge of languages, none of which were English. Various groups of US Army personnel, medics, and others were arriving in jeeps and massive, roaring olive-drab trucks with gigantic white five-pointed stars on the doors all the time.

The first American soldiers we saw on the first day were white; they were in Sherman tanks and the first medics. The first foot soldiers we saw the next morning, though, were black Americans. I'd never seen a black person before, which may sound strange now, but it was true. I later discovered that US intelligence picked up on Germans' unjustified fear of violent, "subhuman" Schwarz Soldaten—black infantrymen—and exploited the prospect of unleashing black American soldiers on German troops to terrify them into surrendering. In an attempt to scare the Nazis into surrender, the Americans distributed flyers depicting black soldiers as bloodthirsty savages willing to castrate weak, defenseless Wehrmacht soldiers. But the black soldiers we met were among the friendliest and most generous people I'd ever encountered.

Convoys of troops arrived to witness the horrors of the camp and assist us in every way they could. Some trucks transported white soldiers, while others transported black soldiers. But we'd never see black and white military working together.

The white Americans were doing everything they could to help us, but I had the impression that some of them didn't want to go too near, to become too connected with us. I suppose I can understand why— we were filthy, strange, desperate creatures infected with who knows what diseases. Typhoid fever had been raging for weeks in the camp, and my friend Ivar had barely survived it. Later, I learned that the American troops had been trained to avoid fraternizing with the locals they encountered throughout the war, to avoid getting sick, to avoid accidental leaks of information that could be useful to the enemy, and to avoid becoming emotionally involved, which would make them less able to do their jobs as soldiers.

But the black soldiers were wonderful to us. It was clear from the start that they were inherently more humane in how they treated us. They gave us every bit of food they could possibly scrounge up and then went looking for more.

Some of them were crying at the horrors they were seeing. Like us, they had been considered inferior beings, subhuman, segregated and given second-class status in their own army, even as they were fighting the Nazi forces whose philosophy was based on a tragic idea of their racial supremacy. There was an instant kinship between us. And that feeling of empathy has remained strong within me ever since.

18

THE VERY FIRST BREAKFAST

Following the roll call, we were led into a makeshift dining hall for our first proper meal. The medics were still being cautious about what and how much they fed us, which was especially necessary given the previous night's catastrophe, in which all of the elderly prisoners had virtually eaten themselves to death.

Each of us received a cup of milk, a little slice of bread, and a single hard-boiled egg. We yelled, screamed, sobbed, and grumbled. It was liberating in and of itself to be able to complain to someone without fear of ending up at the end of a rope or in a ditch with a hole in your head. But no matter how loud we were, that was all we received from the camp cook that first morning.

Following that dinner, as part of the examination of our health status, we all had to wait in line to visit a medic, who tried his best to determine and document the state of our health. I had never experienced puberty since I had been malnourished for so long. My body had never had the extra strength to go through the sexual changes that most normal children go through at a much younger age. I was sixteen years old, but my body belonged to a thirteen-year-old boy. A thirteen-year-old boy who is extremely thin. My weight was 78 pounds. About the size of a healthy German Shepherd.

19

THE FEAR OF FREEDOM

As I gradually regained my strength over the next few days and began to accept the fact that I might actually have a future, I discovered that I was not nearly as pleased as I had anticipated. I was scared. After years in jail, some inmates discover that they have no idea what to do when they are unexpectedly released. Their life in prison may have been dreadful, but at least they were in a controlled atmosphere where they knew the rules. An outside force met their demands, even if that force was harsh in the extreme. And imagine how it played out in my mind if that happened to folks who were fully grown adults when they went to prison and were imprisoned for something they had genuinely done wrong.

I had grown up in the ód ghetto, as well as Auschwitz and Buchenwald. Learning to survive in the concentration camps, one horrible day after another, was the only life I had ever known. As repulsive as it may sound, ód, Auschwitz, and Buchenwald had been my sole homes, and the few people I had made ties with had become my only family.

I was liberated. And completely alone. Of course, there were thousands of people all around me. But, when I stared out from the camp that day at the green, infinite world down the hill, I had no notion what I was going to do or where I was going. I didn't know who I was. I was a naive sixteen-year-old boy. All of the individuals and institutions I had ever trusted in my life had failed to assist me.Germans had attempted to kill me in a variety of ways. They had slain my mother and father, as well as most of my family. Even Allied planes had shot at me and ripped people apart in that blood-soaked boxcar on the route to Buchenwald. These new American soldiers, medics, American Army rabbis, and Jewish social workers appeared to be better than the Germans they had replaced. But I'd been told a thousand times that the folks in charge were on my side and that everything would be great. It had never been true before.

I'd become institutionalized, and strangely reliant on the certainty that I'd be malnourished, brutalized, and persecuted. Even the hell I'd known, my sole reality for all this time, had been snatched away from me. I wasn't the only one who had no idea what the future held. The Americans and their allies were waging a war, and suddenly having to care for tens of thousands of helpless people was not something they had prepared for. They appeared to be doing the best they could given the circumstances, but I was continually concerned that their good nature and intentions would wear off, that they would grow bored of caring for me and the rest of us, and that things would return to normal.

I'd learnt not to trust anyone or anything. That was one of the reasons I survived. And now, just because the uniforms had changed, I was now meant to believe this army, this country, these people who spoke this weird new language? We were in the center of Germany, but the Germans were not going to look after me. They were my tormentors and mortal adversaries. And they were being bombed, shelled, and starving by then. I had no schooling, no family, no money, and no clothes. I didn't even have a home nation to return to. I was already there, at home, and it had done everything it could to destroy me and everyone I had ever known. Years later, I'd discover I'd been suffering from post-traumatic stress disorder. It just felt like soul-numbing, all-encompassing dread at the time.

20

THE LONG WAY

There was a maelstrom of activity around Buchenwald in the early days. There were soldiers all over the place. Truckloads of food and supplies were delivered up the hill from Weimar and unloaded at the kitchen. We'd never seen so much food before: piles upon stacks of flour and sugar, as well as cans of frying oil. Row after row of massive tin milk cartons. There was a Jewish American chaplain in the camp, Rabbi Herschel Schacter, who had arrived just a few hours after the first G.I.s on that first day of release. He did everything he could to organize rescue operations and restore routine and sanity to the camp's Jewish population. Because he spoke Yiddish, he became a sort of go-between for Jews and American military authority. Despite having been raised in the Jewish faith, my later encounters with the Germans had done little to foster faith in a higher force. The Americans were doing everything they could through Rabbi Schacter to help us few remaining Jewish children cope with our trauma and regain some semblance of normalcy and culture. Because Passover was only a week or so before the camp was freed, the rabbi went through the camp handing out matzo, or unleavened bread.

We took full advantage of the chance once we were allowed to eat without restraint. We could eat a dinner that would normally take an hour in a matter of minutes. And I recall never fully believing that there would be food tomorrow, despite the fact that there was plenty of food that day. I couldn't stop myself from hoarding every scrap of food I could get my hands on. At mealtimes, I would pack bread, rolls, and portions of meat into my clothes to ensure I had some later in the evening. I used to hide food under my bed's blankets. We accomplished it all together. I felt bad about doing that. For all these years, I had been trained to be ashamed of everything beneficial for me, anything that would help me live. If I took anything for myself, I was stealing from the Reich, so I was continually looking over my shoulder. Even now, when the generous American G.I.s were more than happy to give us anything they could, we were still acting as if we expected all of our good fortune to vanish at any moment, like a wonderful dream from which you know, somewhere in the back of your mind, you will soon have to awaken. The Americans believed that giving blood transfusions to the worst-off inmates was the best method to treat the severe instances of malnutrition and dysentery, which they performed on a vast scale. Many of the Americans who arrived at the camp ended up in hospital beds for a few minutes, donating blood so that more of us defenseless inmates could live. There was a typhus epidemic in the camp that was still going on when we were liberated. The Americans were quite brave to expose themselves to this disease, and many got infected, but happily they had plenty of the new sulfa treatments that could cure the condition, so it wasn't as horrible for many of them as it had been for us. And, without a doubt, the medications were what saved Ivar. Because the condition affects memory, Ivar had trouble remembering those days for the remainder of his life, despite the fact that he was still sharp and vigorous seventy years later.

The second day of our liberation was a gloomy day for the Americans, who were working so hard to help us and make up for the suffering we had been through in their own way. Though we didn't know much about it, we discovered that their leader and commander had died on that day, April 12, 1945: Franklin Delano Roosevelt, the president who had led America into and through World War II. Without Franklin Roosevelt and the American war effort he built and directed for the whole time I was imprisoned, I would not have survived to tell the tale.

General Eisenhower decided to force German civilians from nearby towns and cities—any civilians within 25 miles—to come up and see what their beloved Führer and their sons, husbands, and brothers had created after witnessing the horrors of the nearby Ohrdruf camp, which had been liberated a few days before, and then witnessing Buchenwald itself. The Germans, largely older, ostensibly respectable folks, were dressed to the nines for the occasion. They formed a lengthy, meandering line that stretched five miles from Weimar's outskirts into and through the camp. The "tour" was designed to leave little to the imagination of the participants. They were forced to look at the stacks of starving, tangled bodies next to the cremation, as well as the half-burned bones still lying within the furnaces. They visited the dreadful barracks where we had been confined for years, five to a wooden rack. And they were forced to breathe in the stench of rotting human flesh and biting chlorine powder; the stench of 21,000 men, all eating, urinating, defecating, and dying in the same little space.

We'd all become accustomed to the stink and horror of what passed for our life after living this way for so long. But these decent Germans, dressed so neatly in their jaunty caps and woolen coats, passed through like wax statues, barely understanding what they were seeing. Some were sobbing and crying in sorrow and disbelief. Some of the women passed out from the shock of seeing and smelling so much horror and death in one area. As the Germans walked by in a slow, solemn procession, it came to me that this had once been my family and myself. My mother and father would have looked right at home, dressed in the same clothes and strolling in the same manner as these folks. Even after all these years of being beaten and starved as a Jew, I remembered that I was once simply a German, like these scared, guilt-ridden Germans descending the hill from their luxurious houses and orderly, immaculate German lives.

21

REMEMBERING THE DEAD

When the camp was liberated, there were hundreds of dead stacked up outside the crematoria for burning. The Germans had departed before they could complete their task of disposing of all of their victims. The dead that had been left in our barracks, near to which we had been sleeping, had also been taken out into the open.

Many people today see the renowned photographs of all those emaciated, tangled bodies as the public face of Buchenwald's liberation. Since freedom, a number of detainees have died, including those who had starved themselves to death. Even though everything conceivable was being done to save them, forty or fifty captives died every day from typhus, dysentery, or sheer malnutrition.

Row after row of the dead had been spread out in a vast clearing. Some of those who perished while the Germans were still in power were naked and exposed to the sky, their garments stripped by guards or even convicts. The recently deceased wore torn clothes, some in the gray-and-blue uniforms of Jewish prisoners from other camps, like myself, and others in the typical street clothes worn by some POWs or political prisoners.

Most of these individuals would be impossible to identify, especially since many of them had been dead for a week or more and were rapidly rotting, their skulls and bones beginning to poke through their skin as it faded away. There was also the issue of typhus and other diseases—something had to be done as quickly as possible about all these rotting remains. So the only option was to bury them in a massive mass grave.

The US Army arrived with bulldozers and excavated a massive ditch in a nearby field. The dead were then shoved in by bulldozers in a massive, toppling heap. There was no other option. But it was terrible.

All of the convicts who wanted to attend the memorial service were gathered by the Americans. I recall the massive earthen mound in front of us, where all those individuals who had once been alive—who had jostled with me for bread—would now rest forever.

Rabbi Schacter read the version of the Kaddish intended for a funeral at a deceased Jew's graveside. The prayer basically says that even if this person—in this case, hundreds of people—died, we still believe in God.

We stood there and spoke the words. But it was just not true for me. How could a God—of all things, a Jewish God—create a world in which all these people, all these Jews, including my mother, father, and sixteen family members, could be swept up and massacred in front of the entire world? What kind of God could have put me through what I had? And then abandoned me in the world, with no family, education, money, home, or country?

I was still alive. That was all there was to it. To be honest, I didn't see much to praise God for. It was up to me to thank for my survival after all those years of anguish and privation. Only this tiny old wise guy, Heinz Adolf Oster, sixteen years old.

I later discovered that I was a member of a very rare club among all the German-born Jewish youngsters who had disappeared into concentration camps during the war—hundreds of thousands of young Jews from Germany and other German-speaking nations. German-speaking Jews were largely Germans or Austrians, with a few Czechs or Lithuanians thrown in as well, and had been picked up in the early years of the Reich when the Nazis began their extermination campaign. This meant that, of all the Jews in the camps, the German-speaking ones had been there the longest. As a result, they had a substantially lower likelihood of survival.

According to reports, only eighteen of the hundreds of German Jewish boys who were put into the camp system survived. Not even enough to occupy a single schoolroom. Not long after our freedom, International Red Cross employees arrived to interview each of us, attempting to comprehend and document who we were, where we came from, and whether we still had any living family.

I recall sitting on my bunk in the former SS barracks, answering question after question in Yiddish while my interrogator scribbled the answers down on his clipboard. I still have his report from that day. It may sound strange, but it felt good to have my life written down—as if I'd stopped being a human being for a while and was now returning to the world of the living.

22

LADIES IN THE BARRACKS

In those first few days of freedom, as our confidence and sense of security grew, we began to be obnoxious in the way that only teenaged boys can. We were a rowdy group of young men at the time. We had little idea of decorum or etiquette. We were like a horde of misplaced boys who had been raised by wolves—very cruel wolves—and then were abruptly pushed back into human civilization. Some psychologists who later studied us thought we were unsalvageable; that we were all so emotionally wounded and damaged that we would all develop into psychopaths with no connection to society and no feelings for anyone but ourselves.

It's difficult to scare a boy who has survived malnutrition, disease, cruelty, and, in my case, a machine-gun firing squad. We were the tough ones, the ones who had made it. Anyone weaker than us had just not made it. So, when we were all crowded together and fed wonderful G.I. food, we started to turn into a very testosterone-addled bunch of kids.

We yelled when we didn't like something. When we weren't stuffing our faces with food, we were strewing it around the camp. With all of this new sustenance entering our bodies, our hormones began to assert themselves in a variety of astonishing ways. Now that my system had the extra calories to spare, I was rapidly maturing from a boy to a man.

I wasn't alone in this. Almost every youngster in the barracks would wake up every morning with a proud, roaring erection, eager to embrace the new day. We'd been squeezed together for years, five on a wooden shelf. We'd been naked together for as long as most of us could remember, on and off. For years, there had been naked males, both dead and alive, all around us, so we didn't feel much shame or embarrassment with each other.

We made up our own little game. We decided to see who was the strongest while racing around in the morning, each of us with our proud, circumcised weiner jutting out.

We'd each take a little bucket and try to hold it up with only our blazing erections. We began to fill the bucket with water to make things more difficult—an empty bucket was not much of a challenge, really. The morning's victor was the child who could hold aloft the bucket the longest while we filled it higher and higher with water.

How did I fare in this strange competition? Let's just say I had my ups and downs. The SS and German Shepherds were no longer there, but life in the barracks remained perilous. We were stranded in the heart of a battle zone, surrounded by gruff, tough men and all manner of terrible weaponry. And, like me and my young friends back in Cologne looking for shrapnel after the air attacks, we were drawn to anything that seemed cool, macho, and deadly.

We weren't the only Jews interested in weaponry there. A week or two after our freedom, a small group of young, serious Jewish guys arrived and began speaking Yiddish to us. These men were strong and healthy, indicating that they had not spent time in the concentration camps. They were very discreet, but they continued asking us where they could get firearms, ammunition, or other weapons. We later discovered that these men were Palestinian Jews and members of the Haganah, the Israeli guerrilla movement that was gathering weaponry all throughout Europe for the war they knew was coming over the establishment of Israel in Palestine.

We didn't have guns, but there were still plenty of ways to get hurt. I recall one miserable boy from Vienna, one of the few German-speaking kids, getting his hands on a German flare from someplace in the camp. He was aware of the presence of a small parachute inside, which was intended to allow the flare to float down once it had been fired into the air. We'd all seen these flares in action, lighting up Auschwitz or Buchenwald whenever there was a nighttime escape or other ruckus.

He began tinkering with it, sitting on his bunk, attempting to figure out how to disassemble it. As he wrestled with it, he pressed the end against his body. It exploded straight in his stomach. He died instantly, his guts spewing all over the room as a result of the explosion. All for the sake of a small parachute.

23

YET ANOTHER TRAIN RIDE

After about a month and a half of growing boredom—just hanging around Buchenwald with no idea what was going to happen to us—the Oeuvre de Secours aux Enfants, or OSE, an international Jewish organization, took over our care and prepared to transport us to the various countries willing to take us in, at least temporarily.

We were obliged to stay in Buchenwald for a variety of reasons. First, the war was still going on, albeit the fighting was shifting eastward as the Americans and British closed the gap against Berlin and the Russian Army rushed west to meet them. And second, the Allies had no idea what to do with us.

Most of us had no family, no homes, and no nation to return to. We'd have to be housed, nourished, and educated before being guided to find our place in a world torn apart by war for six years. Not to mention the hundreds of thousands of war refugees—what Americans termed DPs, or "displaced persons"—who were pushed from their homes and frequently their countries by the destruction of this terrible, all-consuming fight.

At the time, there were approximately 1,000 Jewish orphan boys left in the camp, as Buchenwald had become a gathering place for Jewish boys from other camps throughout Poland and Germany.

Switzerland offered us 280 places. England agreed to admit 250. France took the remaining 427 of us. Rabbi Schacter would follow the delegation to Switzerland, while another American chaplain, Rabbi Robert Marcus, would lead us to France. We were told one glorious morning in early June that we were leaving Buchenwald for good. We were about to board a train bound towards the west.

I packed my meager belongings: a change of clothes and a few trinkets I had collected around Buchenwald since our rescue. I was herded aboard a train once more with the rest of my fellow Jewish orphans. I had no idea where we were heading, where we would end up, or whether things would get better or worse.

After all these years of being herded about like a sheep from bad to worse situations, I had developed a strong dread of the unknown. My impulse was to stay where I was if at all possible, because I had no idea what I might face elsewhere. I'd be dealing with fresh faces, new people, a new nation, and yet another language.

For the first time in many years, I felt somewhat safe at Buchenwald. I didn't want to go. But I didn't have a choice. We didn't have a choice. The OSE was closing down what had become our small haven at Buchenwald, and the Russians were on their way in. Buchenwald was in what was now East Germany, under Russian rule, and our OSE guardians understood we'd be far better off in the West, anyplace in the West, than in the unpredictable, Soviet-dominated East. These OSE members, who are largely young Jewish men,

These OSE people, largely young Jewish men and women, were attempting to assist and care for us. They appeared to be looking out for our best interests. Some of the boys looked to be excited about the new adventure we were about to embark on, or to be putting on their best front; nobody wanted to look scared in front of all his very macho, very competitive friends. Regardless of how many times the OSE staff promised me that everything would be fine, I stepped onboard the train like a cat stepping onto a drowning ship. I was scared.

My family and I had traveled to Łódź by rail. My mother and I were taken to Auschwitz by rail. And a train had brought me, the sole survivor of my family, to Buchenwald. Call me crazy, but I wasn't looking forward to getting on another damned train.

My new life—the terrible, entirely unknown life that lay ahead of me—was waiting for me at the other end of this train voyage. My old life was coming to an end—the life of the boy who had lost practically everything a human being can lose.

As we drove out of the Buchenwald train siding—the same one where I had arrived, almost dead, just a few months before—I attempted to look back, to say farewell in my own confused, addled way. What I was gazing at, craning my neck out the window at Buchenwald's brutal guard towers, muck, and barbed wire, was something altogether else. I instantly understood I was witnessing the end of the abused, malnourished, persecuted youngster I had been for so long. This was the end of the smell, hunger, and horror.

In many respects, I had died, but the mind and body of what was previously known as Heinz Oster were still alive and well, still thinking in my head, still pumping in my heart, still breathing in my chest. I knew, as much as a sixteen-year-old could, that despite the Nazis' torture of my body, I had never really committed myself to them. My humanness. My name, as well as my soul. I remained myself. I was still known as Heinz Adolf Oster.

24

THE RIDE INTO LIFE

As the train gathered speed, roaring through the burned and ravaged German countryside, I slowly shook off my fears. I started to look forward to my new life, though I had no idea of what that life would be. There was plenty of food, much of it handed to us by the American G.I.s as we had prepared to leave the camp. We were each given a basket of provisions to last us through the train ride.

I remember that there were cookies that had been given to a few of the boys, a huge basket of cookies. The G.I.s had assumed that we, like any other civilized group of boys, would share the cookies among ourselves. But sharing was something we had trained ourselves not to do, over our years in the camps. If you had food in your hand you kept it, or only shared with your family or closest friends. When you don't know whether you are going to be fed tomorrow, any food you get is the most precious thing on earth. We had to learn to share again. We had to finally realize that there really was going to be enough food tomorrow, and that if you gave away some of yours today, you were likely to have somebody share something of theirs with you the next day.

Because there was a shortage of good clothing in sizes suitable for the smaller boys, some of us were given leftover Hitler Youth uniforms that the OSE had managed to scrounge somewhere in occupied Germany, with the insignias removed. We were an odd-looking train, to be sure: rebellious, rowdy young men, seemingly taking a carefree holiday through the countryside, dressed in the hated uniforms of the Nazis.

The train, by then, had pretty much turned into a rolling theater. We were traveling through a miserable, defeated Germany, and after all those years in squalor and captivity, we were now free. If anybody could be considered a winner in all this mess, we felt, for the first time in years, a little bit more like winners rather than losers. Some of the kids wrote messages in chalk on the side of the train. We were all slowly coming to the realization that the chances of seeing our families again were very slim. But that didn't calm down the anger that many of us felt against the Germans, and more largely against the world. How could a so-called civilized world allow what happened to us, and our brothers, our sisters, our fathers and our mothers?

One boy, a Pole from Łódź named Joe Dziubak, scrawled a sad question on the side of his train car: "Where are our parents?" it asked in misspelled German. Hundreds of Germans, watching our train chug toward France, were forced to answer his question in their minds. In a larger sense, of course, the question was far simpler: "What have you done, Germany? What have you done?" Other kids wrote taunting messages: "Hitler Kaput" was one of the more popular. Some of the boys ran out and cut down branches from nearby trees when the train stopped. They waved them and shouted to anybody who would listen as we clattered through the countryside.

The going was very slow. The conductor and train engineer had been told to stop and let us enjoy running free in the countryside whenever we wanted, and we wanted to stop and run around every chance we got. We were rediscovering everything. Feeling everything for the first time again. I felt the wet grass between my fingers, inhaled the fresh air and felt the breeze on my skin. I took a moment to look up at the clouds rushing across the sky. Being out there, on my own, felt like running through fields of pure freedom.

Some of the youngsters took advantage of the situation to "liberate" whatever they could get their hands on. There was a strong sense that we were somehow entitled to what we had been denied for so long. Boys returned to the train with a variety of prizes, usually food, but almost anything was fair game. I recall one of the Hungarian youngsters finding a violin, most doubt taken from some abandoned German home, and playing it for hours as the train went on.

To the outside world, we all looked the same: hungry, brutalized children with shaved heads and odd clothing. But there were numerous contrasts between us. We came from various countries. We each spoke a different language. The majority of Poles spoke Yiddish and Polish, while the majority of Hungarians only spoke Hungarian. And we were all emotionally spent. We had no idea how other people felt or how to act in a civilized society. We were nervous, distrustful, and haunted.

Even with all of this newfound happiness and freedom, there was a lot of fighting, usually between Poles and Hungarians. They couldn't converse with one another, and we'd all been schooled in the camps to take everything we could obtain, regardless of how it would affect others. Even with all that food and clothing, we were terrified that this couldn't last—that the only way to survive was to grab anything you could and hang on to it for dear life.

We finally arrived at the border between Germany and France after three days of stop-and-go travel—the train system was still in complete shambles as a result of all the damage done during the battle. I pledged to myself that I would never return to Germany. As the train rattled and roared into France, I took one last good look at the country that had betrayed me.

With a cold wave running through me, I realized I was a boy without a country. I was completely, unequivocally alone.

Most people have a home—a place where they were reared, a comfortable place to return to for comfort, to see old friends and family. To relearn who they were and where they had come from in life. I didn't have anything. Absolutely nothing.

Many good people were doing their best to support us, repair us, make up for all the horrors we had endured, and assist us in coping with what lay ahead. But you can never return to a home that has vanished from the face of the planet, a home that just no longer exists. You can't bring a slain family back to life. After a way of life has been broken, burned, and buried, it cannot be recreated.

Yes, I was still alive. But all I'd been, almost everyone I'd known, was suddenly dissolving into the smoky cloud trailing behind our steam engine, a trail of ash, dust, and cinders that trailed back into Germany.

We were now in France. We were delighted to be there. However, the moment was not as happy as we had anticipated. The war-weary French civilians looked out the train windows at all these yelling, celebrating young men, many dressed up in recycled Hitler Youth uniforms, and assumed we were all little Nazis being transported into France, a country the Nazis had raped and brutalized. The French attempted to attack the train, unaware that we were also victims of the Nazis. To avoid the French crowds that were popping up at the various stops along the way, we were forced to spend one night on a railroad siding outside of Metz.

The OSE chiefs were terrified. The last thing they wanted was for their young charges to be threatened or perhaps beaten because of a dumb misunderstanding about which uniforms we were wearing.

To avoid future mistakes, the OSE leaders scrawled "KL Buchenwald orphans" on the outside of the cars—KL being an abbreviation for the German term Konzentrationslager, or "concentration camp." The statement was written in a combination of German and French: "KL Buchenwald Waisen (orphelins)."

Ivar and I stayed together as our own little fraternity throughout the lengthy train voyage. We were buddies, of course, and had been through so much together that we were like big and small brothers. We were also two of the few youngsters on the train who spoke German—the other guys still referred to us as Yekkes, which is Yiddish for "German." To prevent misunderstandings, anytime someone else was within earshot, we made every effort to speak Yiddish instead, so as not to raise any suspicions among our hotheaded young companions. We didn't have to think too hard about how we would be treated if news got out that we were Germans.

It took another day to travel to Les Andelys, a lovely little village on the Seine river in Normandy, about fifty miles northwest of Paris. From there, we were driven to Ecouis, which was about ten kilometers to the north.

25

WELCOME TO THE ASSISTANCE CENTER

The OSE and the International Red Cross had arranged for us to live in the Normandy countryside. Our new home was a deserted sanatorium on an isolated estate that had been staffed by nuns before the war. The people preparing Ecouis had been told to expect a transport of 427 boys. But nobody had told them that very few younger children had survived any of the concentration camps. So instead of little boys they were faced with a bunch of angry, shaven-headed, ill-mannered teenagers.

Teenagers are pretty high-strung and rebellious in the best of circumstances. If you wanted to create a recipe for making angry, contrary, misunderstood human beings, having your town, your country, your family and your race destroyed while the world seems to do nothing to stop it is a pretty good start. These angry teenagers—like many teenagers throughout human history—didn't care that the authorities, in Ecouis, were sweet people who were doing the best they could to help us. These boys knew their parents had been taken away and probably killed, and that their own lives would never be the same. The world might recover and go on, but for a shaven-headed, scrawny young Jew, with no money, no education, no family and no country, it was easy to feel that things were still pretty bleak. And to feel a lot of stored-up rage.

We were housed in big dormitories with about twenty-five boys in a room. It was the first time I had slept on a real cot that had springs, rather than a wooden platform, ever since my family and I had been taken from our original apartment in Cologne. It doesn't sound like much now, but at the time it was a big event. It made me feel less like a prisoner, a number, a piece of material, and more like a human being. The International Red Cross gave us some new clothing to replace the lice-infested uniforms we had been wearing. To this day,

I still have two pieces of the striped camp uniform I had worn all through Auschwitz and Buchenwald; in Buchenwald, I had found a German military cap which I wore because my head was still shaved. With no hair, your head gets cold pretty easily. In the famous photo of Rabbi Schacter with all the boys who were liberated at Buchenwald, there I am, with my back to the camera, with that same silly cap on my head.

I have two pictures that were taken of me in Ecouis in which I was still wearing that cap. I guess if you have nothing, the smallest things gain a certain importance. It was one thing I could hold on to, no matter where I was taken or what happened to me. We were given delicious food, as only the French could create. I remember that we were each given our own tin cup, and that at every meal—even breakfast—we were served wonderful red French wine. We were poor, homeless kids in a refugee orphanage. But it was France, so we couldn't have a meal without red wine. What a country.

At first, we really didn't know what to do with it—this was the first alcohol we had ever tasted. It was quite a shock to go from starvation to this flood of intense new feelings and wonderful experiences.

Our bodies were being taken care of, but there was still a lot of misery in our hearts. We didn't receive any counseling, per se. And even though we were being fed and clothed very well—as well as anybody could have expected—there was still a lot of anxiety. We just got on with our lives. This was before "post-traumatic stress syndrome" became a common psychological term, but I guess if anyone in history would be likely to suffer from it, it would have been us. Even though we had seen many of these other boys back in Buchenwald, we finally had the time and energy to become close friends with each other.

We had no idea where we were going or what would happen to us when we grew up and had to leave this island of peace and prosperity. So we became friends and commiserate about what we were going to do with the rest of our lives. We were all waiting for word from the Red Cross, which was working around the clock to reunite all of Europe's shattered and ripped-up families.

Nowadays, you'd do all of this with computers and the internet: construct a central database, then enable individuals to find and interact with one another through it. But everything had to be done in person, via hand-carried letters or mail, on a continent that had been bombed, starved, raped, and torn apart by six years of war. I believe there were far over 300,000 Holocaust survivors who needed to be housed, fed, and connected with one another.

It was a slow misery for us homeless youngsters in Ecouis, waiting for word about our families—if we still had them. We were all waiting for someone to take notice of us.

That simply wasn't going to happen for many of us. The only world we knew has vanished. We were the only ones who had survived. But, after a while, that didn't help lessen the anguish of not being wanted. Imagine knowing that no one on the earth genuinely cared about you.

Ivar and I were practically inseparable at the time. We didn't have anyone else, so we became even more like brothers.

We were all asked at one point to declare the country we were from and which country we intended to visit. I selected Palestine because it would accept a refugee like me. I had aspired to see America, but it seemed impossible. My family had tried for years to go there, but we never had the time, money, or opportunity, so what chance did I, a destitute youngster with no schooling, have? Ecouis was never intended to be a permanent residence for anyone. We all understood this was simply a rest stop on the road to—well, we had no idea where it headed. And late at night, alone on your cot, that can be difficult to bear.

As time passed, a few of the lucky lads were reunited with members of their families who had survived, and we said our final goodbyes. We were delighted for them and wished them well. But we never knew what happened to them—they just vanished, like so many of our family and friends before them. For the rest of us, the Red Cross and the OSE knew that we would have to forge our own paths. There would be no one left to help us if our relatives died.

26

SOMEONE ELSE FROM SOMEWHERE

A few of my buddies struck it rich and relocated to Ecouis to live with distant cousins. Several of my friends ended up going to Canada. Some went back to their own countries, while others stayed in France.

The rest of us assumed that because we were already in France and France had volunteered to take us in, we would become French citizens in the future.

This is what happened to Elie Wiesel, another of the Block 66 boys who was imprisoned in the Little Camp during the final days of Buchenwald. He was born in Romania, but after electing to stay in France, which was in much better shape than Romania after the war, he became a French citizen. He also rose to prominence as a writer and was awarded the Nobel Peace Prize. I didn't know Elie's name at the time; he was just another one of "the Boys from Buchenwald."

Going back was pointless if you were Polish or Lithuanian, as Ivar was. The Germans wiped down all Jewish groups and social organizations that had existed for years. If your family had owned a home, you may expect to return to find someone living there who had been assured the house was theirs. There was nowhere to go back to.

When the Polish consul came to visit Ecouis, I told his employees that I was from ód, Poland. I wasn't born there, but I lived there before being sent to Auschwitz and Buchenwald. And, after what Germany had done to me and my murdered family, I refused to be labeled as a German.

This qualified me for an identification card, similar to a passport, proving to the rest of the world that I was from somewhere. My friends, including Ivar, all had their own identity documents, which gave us a little more freedom. A German-speaking youngster with no identity papers would be treated with suspicion in a world full of wandering immigrants and ex-prisoners. The cards gave us the courage to leave Ecouis and venture into the outside world.

In addition, the Polish Embassy gave each of us 500 French francs to spend. It suddenly became clear that I was affluent.

27

WHAT FREEDOM APPEARS LIKE

At Ecouis, I had a lot of free time. We could only learn French so quickly, so the professors and counselors there worked hard to create useful—or at least enjoyable—tasks for us to keep us from concentrating on our pasts or uncertain futures.

We ended up working with our hands, creating arts and crafts out of thin plywood. We cut windmills and little Dutch girls with their pigtails soaring in the air out of paper.

Initially, the teachers divided the boys into age groups. Because that is how pupils are often split, that is how they were accustomed to organizing things. The problem was that we came from such diverse backgrounds, from different nations, and spoke such disparate languages that there were bound to be disputes amongst the various groups. For company and support, we instinctively organized ourselves into what sociologists would call gangs. The difficulty was that forcing members of various gangs to sleep, eat, and attend school together did not work.

The teachers ultimately understood that there was no need to stop us from banding together into our own natural groups. As a result, the Polish kids stayed with the Polish kids, regardless of their age. The Hungarian children formed a group. The older boys naturally assumed the position of big brothers, providing the younger children with someone to guard and instruct them.

We didn't have any families. But, in their stead, we were starting our own families. Ivar and I were like brothers and sisters. Just two fearful youngsters who shared only a few words in our language.

And we shared everything because of what we had both gone through.

There are a few other images from our stay in Ecouis that have survived, showing Ivar and me messing around with our tiny wooden projects. We almost appear to be regular, cheerful young males with nothing better to do but carve wood with a jigsaw. I got bored of doing what the teachers asked me to do one day. After a while, it just didn't have much meaning. Our instructor instructed me to create whatever I desired. But I had no idea what she was talking about.

"Tell me about how you felt when you were liberated," he urged.

At first, I didn't comprehend him.

"Tell me how it felt." "How it appeared on the inside."

I remembered those last, sweltering days in Block 66, when I had to breathe via a tiny window at the roof's peak. I remembered the terrible odor of rotting carcasses and choking chlorine. I informed the instructor that freedom meant bursting through the barrier between me and the air, between me and the sun. I created a rough wooden sculpture of a youngster with his arms outstretched, feeling the light and the air while a wall collapses in front of him. I constructed a yellow-painted plastic sun that shined brightly outside the walls.

28

EXODUS OF THE GOOD SHIP

Bricha—"flight" in Hebrew—was a covert operation that was gathering traction to convey homeless Jews from Europe to Palestine. Millions of Jews were interned in displaced persons camps. Following the Holocaust, the surviving Jewish people were resolved to create their own homeland so that nothing like what had happened would ever happen again. Because most Jews were not permitted to migrate to British-controlled Palestine, an underground coalition of Jewish leaders and warriors, including the Haganah, was formed to assist in smuggling displaced Jews into what would later become Israel.

I didn't have a country to move to, so when Bricha members showed up at Ecouis to attempt to recruit Jews to come and help create Israel, I agreed. I had a ticket on the soon-to-be-famous SS Exodus 1947 to travel from France to Palestine. This ship was intended to be the site of a conflict between Jews seeking to travel to Palestine and the British authorities in power at the time. The British did not desire a wave of Jewish migrants, the majority of whom lacked legitimate immigration papers. The Arabs and Palestinians who lived in Palestine were also unimpressed with the proposal.

However, the Haganah, the armed wing of the Israel-creation movement, sought to force the world to notice the atrocities Jews were still facing. So they were ready to sail this ancient second-hand ship from France to Israel, daring the British to stop them with force and exposing the world to yet another image of Jews being pushed around and mistreated. As our time there dragged on, the Ecouis officials determined that if we were going to remain there much longer, we needed a job, and began to provide us with the education we needed to succeed. What did I aspire to be? To begin my schooling, I needed to pick what I wanted to do with the rest of my life. My true ambition was to become a comedian. Throughout all of my terrible situations and madness, I always seemed to be the one who tried to lighten the mood—to make something a bit funny out of any situation. When everyone around you is in a terminal depression, a condition of perpetual pessimism—in our friends' and families' cases, for very valid reasons—being the funniest guy in the room isn't that difficult.

Of course, a lot of my wit sprang from the fact that I didn't know any better. I had no idea how horrible things were. "You're so damned funny," people would say to me. You should try your hand at stand-up comedy." And after enough of this, I began to believe them over time. Of course, I lacked any actual talent or expertise in that area: it's one thing to make your friends and family laugh, but it's quite another to stand in front of a room full of strangers and make them laugh every time, day after day. And the professors at Ecouis, like most knowledgeable teachers and parents around the world, were skeptical that being a comic would be a viable career for me.

Although it was not my first choice, I began training to become a civil engineer, the folks who design and build bridges, roads, and tunnels. I wasn't thrilled with the concept. It didn't appear to be nearly as much fun as hanging around in cabarets and nightclubs, making everyone laugh while the girls in the audience admired me. At least, that's how the story went. Unlike many of the lads, I could read and write in German and Hebrew, which I had learned while studying for my clandestine bar mitzvah. But definitely not in French. I had a lot of work ahead of me. So I enrolled in civil engineering school. For one day only.

29

THE AMERICAN MALE

On the afternoon of my first day of training, I arrived home from engineering school to find a civilian waiting for me. He presented himself and stated that he was the vice-consul of the United States from the American embassy in Paris.

He told me in French that the Red Cross had uncovered a link after taking all the information I had given them back in Buchenwald—the names and addresses of all the relatives I could remember.

They had researched my uncle's name—Herbert Haas, one of my mother's brothers—and my memories of him living in Philadelphia.

"I'm afraid I have to tell you," he said, "your uncle Herbert no longer lives in Philadelphia." Regardless, he came upon your name in a Los Angeles newspaper. "The Red Cross has asked for the names of survivors like you to be published in newspapers all over the world." B'nai B'rith, which translates to 'Sons of the Covenant' in Hebrew, is a Jewish daily newspaper published in Los Angeles, California. Your uncle came upon your name in the newspaper. And he is eager to welcome you into his family, even inviting you to visit him and his wife in the United States."

It marked a turning moment in my life. It was the beginning of my life. I couldn't stop giggling. Someone wanted me to go somewhere out there. I couldn't believe this was happening after years of being abandoned by nearly every institution I'd encountered. When it appears like the entire world has turned its back on you for all those years, you begin to believe that you do not deserve to be considered a human being.

After being constantly shattered and feeling worthless for so long, now this? I was almost insane with happiness. Who would have guessed that after all of this, I'd wind myself in America—a land of pure fantasy, a country where almost everyone in the world aspired to live? It was a miracle that happened to me, as it had happened to so many others throughout the years. That afternoon, my journey to Palestine was canceled. I had no desire to travel to what could be another long battle with both the British and the Palestinians when I could instead travel to America.

I ended up donating my Exodus ticket to another Ecouis acquaintance.

Even though I knew where I was headed, I had to figure out how to get there. There were no civilian passenger ships traveling from France to America so soon after the war: every available ship was crammed with returning American and Canadian troops.

Even if there had been a ship, how could a poor Jewish orphan finance the journey? My uncle Herbert and aunt Bertha didn't have any money, and neither did I. It would be months before I could even think about visiting the United States.

30

IN PARIS, A FREE MAN

Ecouis was later closed down as many of the inmates found other places to live, and separate groups of the inmates of Buchenwald were moved to other sites in France.

I ended up at an estate held by the Rothschilds, who were once the richest family in the Western world. They had offered to host a group of orphans at one of the several estates they owned throughout Europe.

This sounded great—until we arrived. Instead of living in opulence in one of the Rothschilds' estates, we were shoved into the servants' quarters, deep in the back of the place where guests and relatives would never go.

The servants' quarters were dirty and falling apart, and you can believe that if you hear it from someone who escaped Auschwitz. I ended up getting scabies from the filthy bedding and linens. It's caused by a mite that penetrates the skin and multiplies beneath the surface, and it's the most dreadful, itchy thing you can imagine. It was so severe that I had to be brought to a hospital in Paris to be treated.

But even this worked out in my favor—though it would have been difficult to persuade me of that at the time, given that the therapy required me to take a searing, toxic bath twice a day, which stained my skin purple. Every time I had to go through it, I felt like a Smurf.

The good news was that during my therapy, I met a wonderful French nurse named Carmen. She was one of the women who helped me bathe, so you could say I didn't keep any secrets from her.

I was freed from the hospital and relocated to a new house in Champigny-sur-Marne, on the southeast outskirts of Paris, once I was cured and no longer purple all over.

There were always two cartons of cigarettes in the envelopes that my uncle sent to me. Which was amazing because, even though I didn't smoke—I nearly passed out when I tried—these smokes were like money in those days of deprivation and rationing.

I also had some extra cash in my pocket, so I was able to go out on the town and buy a few things. And my new companion Carmen was a smoker, so having cigarettes definitely made me appear more appealing than I otherwise would have.

Of course, I kept in touch with Carmen, and one night after we saw a movie, she invited me to her room in the nurses' dormitory. She was incredibly nice. She was really proud of her violin skills and insisted on performing for me. She had put down the violin, shut off the lights, and taken me to bed before I knew it. For the first time in my life, we made love. She was extremely kind, patient, and understanding. It was a fantastic introduction to the world of sexual pleasure, and a stark contrast to where I had been and what I had been through: just a few months before, I had been starving in Buchenwald; now, I was larking around Paris with a few francs in my pocket, and I was even sleeping with my own French girlfriend.

Even now, I joke that when I hear a violin, I can feel something stirring...

I and the other Champigny-sur-Marne boys enjoyed wandering around Paris. It seemed like I was in heaven. Many of Paris' most popular attractions, such as the shows at the Folies Bergère and the Moulin Rouge, were free for us. We were handed a fantastic green pass that read, in French, "Extend any Courtesy to Veterans and Ex-Prisoners."

My friends and I could go to the movies and shows whenever we pleased. It nearly seemed too good to be true. It was a nice introduction to the delights of living in the free world, drinking wine and seeing gorgeous French dancers. And it was at the Folies Bergère that I saw a naked lady for the first time in my life—all of Carmen's exploits had occurred in the warm, beautiful darkness of her dorm room.

One night, a group of friends and I boarded the train to Pigalle, the city's famous theater and red-light district, to catch a movie double feature. Gunga Din starred Cary Grant, Douglas Fairbanks Jr., and Sam Jaffe, a charming Jewish youngster who played the title role as a wretched Indian water bearer. We also saw The Four Feathers, a film starring C. Aubrey Smith about the British soldiers causing havoc in another country.

When the movie ended, our little gang spilled out into the streets, taking in all the lights, sounds, and unfettered life that was going on around us. We weren't looking for prostitutes, at least not to use their services. We had no idea what a prostitute was. We were so naïve and wet behind the ears that all we knew was that they were evil women.

31

IN PARIS, A FREE MAN

On another, nicer day, Ivar and I went for a stroll along the gorgeous Avenue des Champs-Élysées, the vast, light-filled boulevard that leads to the Arc de Triomphe, the iconic arch at the top of the long hill. We stopped at one of the many cafés along the avenue for coffee and something sweet. The waiter approached us while we were conversing in German or Yiddish, depending on who was speaking.

"Pardon me," he apologized. "Pardon the interruption, but there is a gentleman a few tables over who overheard you speaking German and would like to meet you young men." Mr. and Mrs. Rosenthal were introduced to us as a German Jewish couple who had escaped Nazi Germany to France in 1937 and had managed to hide from the Germans throughout the war.

He turned out to be a French Ministry of Transport official, out of all the persons we could have met in France. This was the man who could assist me get out of France and across the Atlantic to America. Mr. Rosenthal and his wife adopted me in a manner after our meeting at the café, and over the following few weeks I went over to their house in Paris for Friday dinners, getting to know them and their family.

As time passed, a plan was devised to bring me over the Atlantic. Mr. Rosenthal discovered that he had a brother who lived in Los Feliz, a nice palm-tree-lined neighborhood in the north-central part of Los Angeles, California, and he had been looking for a way to send money to his brother without the red tape and expense of sending it to him from France. Mr. Rosenthal offered that my uncle, who was already in Los Angeles, would transfer the money for my ship journey to his brother in Los Feliz, and that he would then buy me a ticket to the States here in Paris.

He also pulled some strings and arranged for my passage aboard the Desiré, a rusty freighter sailing from Normandy to New York. It was one of the first ships after the war to transport passengers from France to New York. And now, out of all the migrants in Europe, I had a golden ticket to join them. I bid Ivar farewell. I was unsure whether I'd ever see him again. He was heartbroken to see me depart, and I believe it must have been terrible for him to say goodbye to the older brother who had attempted to look after him since Buchenwald. But we both realized I needed to go. There was no doubt about that. Ivar was in good hands in Paris, swiftly learning French and receiving a good education. I had a family and possibly a good new life across the seas.

We pledged to keep in touch, even though we both realized it would be difficult given how messed up the world was at the time. It was difficult to say goodbye to my one true friend in the world. But I didn't have much of a choice. I was gone. I bid my other friends and teachers farewell and boarded a train in Paris bound for the port of Cherbourg. Paris had escaped destruction during the war, but Cherbourg, the closest port to the D-Day landings in Normandy, had been bombarded by the Allies from the air, sea, and ground, and there was war debris and antiquities everywhere. We were dodging lingering German mines as the ship left Cherbourg harbor. The crew even fired at some of them, attempting to blow them up before they could blow us up. We were soon on the open Atlantic, thumping along with a trail of black oil smoke, destined for New York City, and none of them went off.

32

THE GIRL IN THE HARBOR

When you land in New York on a broken-down ship and view the Statue of Liberty, it's an almost indescribable experience. I don't care how many others have attempted to tell it, but seeing that impossible statue, with that torch lifted high in the air, changes everything. Everything you are, who you are, and everything you have been through all shift totally at that moment. That fantastic, beautiful, symbolic edifice informs you that you have arrived at the gates of something beyond your wildest imagining.

People born in America have no idea what America means to poor, battered, desperate people who have run out of luck, money, or space wherever they came from. America is much more than a new location to these people—people like myself on that dismal day in April 1946. It is a new beginning. I didn't have much money. I couldn't communicate in English. I possessed no abilities. I had nowhere to live and no genuine family. Even though I arrived with nothing, I felt like the luckiest kid on the planet. After being reviled and nearly annihilated by the Nazis for so many years, having so many things go well in my life seemed like a long, glorious dream.

It's a dream from which I've yet to awaken all these years later. I remained in New York for a brief time with a distant relative, Millie Lachman, a cousin of my mother, and her husband, Henry, whom I had met in Germany. I also reconnected with a couple of Cologne friends. One was a child my age who was the son of one of my mother's cousins, and the other was an old classmate of mine from before the Germans kicked us out of school in 1935. These amazing people gave me my first impressions of America. The sight of my first American store practically knocked me over. There was nothing like this in Europe: everyone shopped at a small store within walking distance of their houses. This was a church dedicated to food in all of its forms. Bread fortifications. Milk in vast quantities. A meat counter larger than any I'd ever seen. Fresh, vibrant green veggies and a rainbow of fruits from throughout the world.

Another American creation that stole my breath away was the Automat. It appears eerie and industrial now, yet it was a remarkable idea at the time. You inserted your 50 cents into a slot and then reached inside a whirling machine to select your sandwich. It was mechanical and robotic, yet it was also hip, current, and fast. You could obtain a sandwich in a matter of seconds instead of waiting for an actual person to take your order, assemble your meal, and then take your money and make change. Things happened in America faster than everywhere else on the planet. All of this cuisine was a visual pleasure, as well as an eye-opening glimpse of a whole new world, the world of the future, unfolding right in front of my astonished eyes. However, the dish itself did not excite me in any way. Even now, when people meet me and learn what I went through all those years ago, they seem to have an insatiable desire to feed me. "You were starving," they'll tell you. "You need to eat a little more."

I'm sorry to disappoint these well-meaning individuals, but food doesn't mean much to me. It hasn't happened since I left Buchenwald. That was back in the day, and this is now. I can't make up for what I didn't get back then. It's possible that my stomach and metabolism grew up with little to no food, and that this never changed after I moved to America, the capital of too-much-to-eat. I don't want to eat a lot at once, and eating, cleaning up, and digesting may be such a chore that I wish I didn't have to do it at all.

33

AT LAST, I AM HOME

When I arrived in Los Angeles, my uncle Herbert and aunt Bertha were overjoyed to see me, adopt me, and assist me in starting a new life in America.

But it was clear from their expressions that they pitied me as well. Compared to all the healthy, milk-fed people in Los Angeles, I was a skinny, pitiful-looking thing. "You're so pale!" people would say. "You're so thin!" when I was actually looking amazing in comparison to how I had looked only a few months earlier.

I started out a little taller than most of the other lads, but my body was doing everything it could to catch up. My physique grew like a sunflower plant once I moved to California and began to live a more regular life. In one year, I grew four inches.

My aunt and uncle bought me my very first complete suit. I was quite pleased with it. However, I was never able to wear it in public. My arms were jutting out of the sleeves like the wooden arms of a scarecrow by the time a family wedding prompted me to put it on.

I was relieved to be expanding, but it was agonizing. My joints were aching all the time, as they were going through the growing pains of those lost years in a matter of months. My body felt as if it no longer fit me.

My aunt and uncle could not have been more friendly or loving. In retrospect, it seems that they poured all those years of yearning to be parents into me because they had not been prepared to have their own children, because of all the traumas they had endured. They probably tried to spoil me.

Some of my current friends and family may believe they have succeeded. My aunt had been compelled to do piecework at a textile factory in Philadelphia to make ends meet, sewing uniform jackets for American soldiers. My uncle, Herbert, had not been able to receive an education before leaving for America, like the rest of us German Jews, but he loved cars—he had raced cars back in Germany, and he had been injured in a crash when he was young. He had a huge scar on his cheek from the accident that he had to wear for the rest of his life. Back in Germany in the 1930s, the only job he could find was as a salesman for Opel, which is today General Motors' German division. Then he married my aunt Bertha and relocated to Cologne, my hometown. As a Jew, he was not permitted to run his own business, so he was forced to work in a garage on other people's cars.

He did the same thing when he moved to America: he owned an Atlantic Richfield gas station—now known as ARCO—on Wilshire Boulevard in downtown Los Angeles, directly adjacent to Good Samaritan Hospital.

He was working at his petrol station when the owner of the B'nai B'rith Messenger, a well-known historic Jewish newspaper in Los Angeles, stopped by. This man was a regular at Uncle Herbert's gas station, and he knew Herbert was looking for any members of his family who had survived the lunacy in Europe.

Every Friday, when the paper came out, dad would stop by my uncle's gas station on the way home, fill up with Atlantic Richfield gas, and give my uncle a free copy of the paper. And that's how my uncle found out I was still alive: by accident, a publisher dropped off a certain paper, on a certain Friday, with my name on a list of concentration-camp survivors.

When I moved to Los Angeles, I quickly realized that running a petrol station was not a good way to make a living. My uncle was not the owner—oil corporations had to lease their stations to operators like him. Atlantic Richfield was in charge of everything. Uncle Herbert barely made three or four cents on the dollar each gallon of fuel. He was only able to sell Pennzoil oil and Goodyear tires. To supplement his income, he repaired his customers' vehicles, including repairs, oil changes, chassis lubrication, tires, wiper blades, and brake-shoe replacements. That money was his to retain for his effort and the tiny profit on the parts.

Uncle Herbert's station was in a bad neighborhood. Wilshire Boulevard was a well-traveled thoroughfare in this enormous, bustling city, but it was not where many people resided, so people were hurrying by on their way to and from work when they passed his station and were not eager to stop and have their cars serviced there. It was difficult going. My new adoptive parents had been compelled to borrow money to post a bond for me, to demonstrate to the government that they had sufficient finances to care for me and that I would not be a drain on the system here. They were then required to repay that money, month by month, on top of what it actually cost us to live.

My new family never had enough money to do anything other than stay at home and work. I was able to accumulate enough money at one point to take my adoptive parents to San Diego and stay at the Coronado Hotel. I also took them to Lake Tahoe, which is located in the mountains on the boundary of California and Nevada. But these were extremely unusual and extraordinary events.

Uncle Herbert and Aunt Bertie resided in Hollywood in a rented property, a modest little one-story California bungalow. They only had one bedroom. So, just like previously, I had to sleep in the living room, pulling out the foldable sofa bed every night throughout my trips. And that's where I slept every night from 1946 to the early 1950s. I had to go to school, of course. And, having not attended school since 1935, I had a lot of catching up to accomplish. To begin, I didn't know a single word of English. Yes, German. Yes, Yiddish. A touch of Polish. But there is nothing more difficult in English than "Hello" and "Goodbye." Thousands of children arrived in the city after the war, displaced people from all over the world who needed to be taught in Los Angeles. To make things easier for everyone, we were all placed at Belmont High School, despite the fact that none of us spoke English. There, instead of the typical one-hour session, we could get three hours of English teaching every day, giving us a fighting chance of catching up to all these native California pupils.

Every morning, I had to take the streetcar down Beverly Boulevard from our bungalow in Hollywood to high school. By chance, the school was approximately five or six blocks from my uncle's gas station.

Every day after school, I walked to the station and worked from 3:30 p.m. to midnight. My uncle taught me how to run the station, sell petrol, and keep the books, as well as conduct some of the simpler repairs and service for his customers' automobiles. When my shift was through, he would come and pick me up. He would sometimes arrive early and stay with me after dinner to keep me company so I could do my homework at the gas station office. This allowed him to save the money he would have spent on employing someone to manage the station when he wasn't there, so at the very least I had a chance to enrich their life a little—to repay my aunt and uncle for their incredible love and support. It felt wonderful to know that I was repaying them for all of their efforts in taking me in and raising me, as well as the money they had spent to provide me a new life.

Uncle Herbert had saved enough money after a few years for us to move to a bigger, nicer place up on Genesee Street in Hollywood. I now have my own bedroom, complete with a wooden frame, a spring basis, a mattress, and everything. It was the first time since 1935 that I had my own proper bed. It may appear insignificant, but it meant a lot to me at the time. I was suddenly a genuine person who, like everyone else, deserved a proper bed. That's how I lived for ten years, working every night at my uncle's gas station through high school and college. It took me ten years to get from homeless, skinny German Jewish refugee to Californian. My aunt had insisted that I work hard, attend a respectable college, and find a job that would allow me to use my brain. She wasn't going to allow me to lose out on the opportunity that had been presented to me by traveling to America and California.

"If you've come this far and survived everything," she said, "you have to do something special with the gifts you've been given."

She didn't want me to end up like my uncle, a beautiful man who made a life off of oil changes and tire rotations, coming home every night with axle grease and nasty oil under his fingernails. She didn't have to work very hard to persuade me. Whereas many of the boys I went to high school with became distracted by owning cars, chasing girls, drinking beer, and screwing about, I took things a little more seriously.

Many of the lads I knew—mostly other European Jewish survivors who had immigrated to California after the war, like me—seemed to become caught up in their current lives and aspirations, without worrying about their futures. They weren't as invested in their studies and their future as I was. I suppose you can't blame them. They had come from so little and had arrived with almost nothing in many cases. They wanted to live their lives at full speed right then and there. They wanted to have fun, go crazy, have girlfriends, get married, and have babies right immediately.

But, after all that turmoil, I believe I was committed to being the master of my own fate from then on. I'd already been destitute, malnourished, and subjected to the whims of some really terrible individuals, in my opinion. I wanted to be in charge of my own life from then on. I wanted this narrative to have a happy conclusion if I could help it.

I was in a rush. I graduated from Belmont High academic in two and a half years, partially because I arrived in the middle of the first academic year, in 1946. I graduated among the top 3% of my class. Of course, the fact that I was eighteen years old when I started, rather than the customary fourteen or fifteen, helped. When I graduated, I was already twenty-one years old. As a result, I was far more mature than most of the other students in my classes. I also studied hard, foregoing some of the social pleasantries that had distracted some of my Belmont High classmates. But now that I'd accomplished these goals—learning English and graduating from high school with honors—what was I going to do with the rest of my life?

34

WELCOME TO WESTWOOD

I chose to attend UCLA for college—or, rather, my circumstances chose for me. We still didn't have a lot of money. I needed to attend a local college in order to continue living with my aunt and uncle and working at my uncle's gas station. He needed me there, and that was the only way I knew to get some money to help fund my college education.

In comparison to some of the city's more exclusive and distinguished private universities, UCLA was comparatively inexpensive. And UCLA was quite open to international students of all colors and backgrounds. People flocked from all over the world to attend UCLA, as they still do today. There were many Jewish youngsters like me—refugees and survivors—so I'd have no trouble making friends with whom I'd have a lot in common.

UCLA was not an easy place for me. One English teacher ordered me to come into his office because "I cannot pass you with the kind of mistakes you are making with the language."

He had made so many red marks on my papers that they resembled red-and-white barber poles when he handed them back. I attempted to explain, but he interrupted me.

"You have an accent." "Were you not born here?" he inquired.

"No," I responded, "I've only been here since 1946."

He gazed at me for a few seconds. "Why didn't you tell me this?" he questioned. "You can't learn English as a second language that quickly when all these other kids have been speaking it since birth."

He agreed to give me extra attention and to lower my mark because I had only recently heard, let alone spoken, this new language.

But what did I aspire to be? I still wanted to be a comic in the back of my mind, but it wasn't a practical objective. I talked with a German accent, which isn't a good foundation for comedic material after WWII. And my background—well, it didn't seem like talking about my experiences as a Holocaust survivor was a sure-fire way to garner laughs night after night.

I was spending a lot of time at the dentist at the time. The malnutrition I had endured had hampered the growth of my teeth: my teeth and gums were simply not the same size, and it appeared that I would end up with dentures instead of my own teeth.

But I discovered a fantastic dentist who accepted me as a challenge. I attended two or three times a week, doing my best to rehabilitate my teeth. My teeth ended out well in the end—I still have them, after all these years. My dentist and I became good friends, and it looked like an interesting way to make a career. So I opted to pursue a pre-med program at UCLA, gaining the education and qualifications required to enter dental school.

I got my first car somewhere along the way, a fairly used 1936 Ford sedan with a soft top. It wasn't a convertible, but it did have a cloth roof rather than a steel one. Every time it rained, the ridiculous top splashed water on my head, papers, and books.

My uncle had a lot of opportunities to buy used cars at low prices—customers were frequently coming in, attempting to get rid of their cars in order to afford a nicer, newer one. So we sold the Ford and bought a cool little '39 Chevy convertible in blue, which matched the UCLA school colors. When I wasn't in college, I worked at a petrol station. With the exception of Saturday afternoons. That's when my uncle hired a part-time employee to manage the station so I could go to UCLA football games like every other carefree, fun-crazed American kid. My pals and I got right into the spirit of things. We'd decorate my Chevy with blue-and-yellow flags, ribbons, and pom poms. We drove through Westwood and all over campus, blasting the horn and screaming anytime UCLA won a game.

35

SORRY. WAY TOO JEWISH

There was no acknowledgement that it had arrived, no indication that it was valued. Dr. Rutherford informed me during my interview, "You know, I'm sure you've heard through the grapevine that we rarely accept anybody the first year they apply—we have so many students backlogged." However, because you have already applied and met all of the conditions, we will keep your name on the list of applicants. We'll just keep it in the hopper. As a result, you will not have to repeat the process. We will contact you. We'll consider you again next year, but with the advantage of being that much higher up the list, so you'll have a much better chance of being admitted."

Dr. Rutherford stood up and excused himself from the interview at one point to attend to another subject. I had a look at my application materials, which were sitting on his desk. And across the top of the cover was written: "Germ Jew."

"German Jew," to put it another way.

That gave me a horrible feeling.

I hadn't given it much attention at the time—I'd been treated so well throughout America, through high school and college in California, that I'd forgotten antisemitism was still a problem. In other words, I was gullible.

USC was founded as a Methodist Christian college and had a long history of not accepting Jews. Before the war, there was a very precise numerus clausus, or quota program at USC: each year, one

Jewish student was accepted to the medical school, one to the dental school, and one to the law school.

I had no idea that Rufus Bernhard von KleinSmid, the president of USC until 1947, was a co-founder of the Human Betterment Association. This organization promoted the odd eugenics and forced sterilization practices that the Nazis employed as a "scientific" justification for segregating, sterilizing, and eventually exterminating the mentally ill, homosexuals, and Gypsies. Not to mention millions of Russians and six million Jews, including the majority of my family and nearly myself.

Von KleinSmid and his colleagues' perverted views pushed more than thirty jurisdictions, including California, to allow forced sterilization of the "feebleminded and insane." As I previously stated, approximately 60,000 persons were sterilized as a result of these legislation, with California accounting for one-third of them.

"The application of eugenics principles to organized society is one of the most important duties of the social scientist of the present generation," von KleinSmid stated in a 1913 paper presented to the Cincinnati Academy of Science. "We must all agree that those who, by definition, can do little more than pass on to their offspring (sic.) the flaws that make them burdens on society have no ethical right to parenthood."

As of 2014, the USC website featured a historical chronology that includes Doctor von KleinSmid, "affectionately known as Dr. Von," becoming President of the University in 1921. He retained that position until 1947, just six years before I applied to the University of Southern California's School of Dentistry.

Von KleinSmid was not alone in his erroneous — and eventually genocidal — views. The Human Betterment Association included Stanford University's first president, David Starr Jordan, Los Angeles

Times publisher Harry Chandler, and Nobel Prize-winning physicist Robert A. Millikan. Adolf Hitler utilized these viral views about certain individuals being innately inferior to others to justify his efforts to murder millions of innocent people.

But I didn't realize this when I was applying to USC's dental program. All I knew was what Dr. Rutherford had informed me: I would be considered for admission the following year.

Around July of that year, I began to get concerned. Acceptances for admission to dentistry school were generally sent out in May or June, but it was almost summer and I had not heard from them.

I rescheduled an appointment with Dr. Rutherford. And it immediately became evident that, despite what he had indicated the previous year, he had no intention of accepting me. "Well, Henry," he replied, looking me in the eyes, "you didn't make another application."

"No, because I actually trusted you," I replied. You stated you'd leave me 'in the hopper' with the applicants from last year."

"Well," he replied. "You should have still made a new application."

I knew I was doomed. I was beyond frustrated and enraged. I had worked so hard and gone through all of these tests and examinations, only to discover that USC would not admit me as a Jew to their dentistry program.

I stormed out of USC, walked down Jefferson Boulevard to the Southern California College of Optometry, and applied the same day.

Despite the fact that the names were similar, the college was unrelated to USC. It was a whole different company. And I must say, they treated me far better than USC ever did.

At the moment, I had no idea what optometry was. I'd never worn glasses, and I'd never had an eye checkup in my life. But I had a UCLA acquaintance who said he was going there after graduation to become an optician. He was an extremely bright young man who excelled in school. "Well, this is a smart guy, and if he wants to be an optometrist, maybe I do, too," I reasoned. "What have I got to lose?"

I strolled in, grabbed an application form, and completed it.

Three weeks later, I got accepted to optometry school. Please forgive me for this scary pun, but I've never regretted that decision. I graduated, became a Professor of Optometry at the same school, maintained my own optometry office for 56 years, and worked as a staff optometrist for Kaiser Permanente until 2014.

During the war, the Nazis made a point of removing the eyeglasses of concentration-camp inmates in order to make them feel helpless and less likely to rebel or flee. So it always seemed a little ironic to me that I'd spend my life as an optometrist, helping thousands upon thousands of people improve their lives. To assist people in seeing their loved ones, participating in sports, learning from literature, viewing great works of art, watching inspiring movies and attending spectacular theatrical performances, as well as experiencing the natural marvels of the amazing planet we live on.

My wife Susan and I like traveling as much as we can in our spare time. Las Vegas is one of our favorite vacation spots. I enjoy a little gambling: playing poker and the occasional slot machine. After the life I've led—where I began, what my family and I went through, and where I ended up—I'm shocked I can still enjoy myself every day, that I can still get up and feel the joy of life after all these years. I can't help but think I'm a tiny bit lucky.

36

GO BACK TO GERMANY

When I boarded a train to France in 1945, I resolved never to return to Germany for the rest of my life. I kept my promise for nearly seventy years. There was a time when I was compelled to do a short layover in Frankfurt, Germany, on a journey to another location in Europe. I joked with my family and friends that I was attempting to float above the floor by walking on my toes while waiting for my connecting flight out of the country.

Then, a few years ago, my wife Susan's cousin was on his computer, looking at a map of Cologne, Germany—my birthplace and hometown. He was using OpenStreetMap, an online software that is similar to Google Maps and Wikipedia in that it can display information that people submit superimposed on a searchable map of the world. He summoned me to examine a smattering of orange spots dispersed over the metropolis. They were the locations of little brass-covered stones known as Stolpersteine, or "stumbling blocks," which had been embedded in the sidewalks.

Gunter Demnig, a Cologne artist, had devised an ongoing project to remind Germans of what they had done—and to honor the innocent Holocaust victims—by placing brass-covered stones in front of the last dwelling from where each victim was removed. The "stumbling stones" were inspired by an anti-Semitic German custom of declaring, "There must be a Jew buried here," anytime someone tripped over a jutting cobblestone. It's a prejudiced, backhanded joke about how all Jews have huge noses, and it means "If it's annoying, a Jew must be the cause."

Demnig flipped this habit on its head by placing these stones such that they protrude from the surrounding sidewalk, making it more likely that you will trip over them. He transformed it from a snide remark into a constant reminder of Germany's guilt and responsibility—a constant, permanent tribute to what the German people did to Jews and other oppressed minorities.

We discovered that Stolpersteine had erected a tribute to my parents in front of our last apartment in Cologne, at 15 Blumenthalstraße.

It was a remarkable and distressing experience to see that someone—a German, no less—had gone out of his way to make tributes for my mother and father. It brought it all back to me, like a crashing wave at Sunset Beach, my memories of my family, my house, my relatives, and all the horrors we had gone through.

I was grateful to Gunter Demnig and the staff at the Cologne museum who had assisted him in uncovering and documenting the experiences of all the victims, Jewish and non-Jewish, who had been dragged from their homes and slaughtered.

But I had a couple of ideas, which neither my friend and co-author, Dexter, nor my wife, Susan, were surprised by.

The stones for my parents were erected in front of the apartment building we were forced to live in when the Nazis took control. I didn't consider this place to be my home. It felt more like the first prison we'd been put into, at the start of all this lunacy. Instead, if it had been up to me, I would have had my parents' memorial placed in front of our own home at 12 Brabanterstrasse.

I also observed that the information on my mother's stone was incorrect. It is said that she, along with my father, were slain in ód. That was all everyone knew about what had happened to her—except me, of course. My father's death was documented in the ód ghetto medical records, but the Germans destroyed all evidence when they carried her and me from Łód to Auschwitz. And they surely never recorded what happened to her that first night at Birkenau—as far as the rest of humanity knew, she was borne away by the wind.

I emailed the National Socialist Documentation Center of the City of Cologne, or NSDOK, in an attempt to amend the record of what had occurred to my parents and myself. Trying to contact Germans about what Germany had done to my family seemed odd.

Dr. Karola Fings, a remarkable researcher, author, and historian who has dedicated her career to unearthing the truth about what happened during those dark years and teaching Germans and the rest of the world, called. I realized that the Germany I knew—the Germany that had caused so much murder, pain, and devastation—was not the Germany of today.

Dr. Fings' work, and the work of all her colleagues, is based on a single simple principle: that the only way for humanity to prevent a horror like the Holocaust from happening again is to force ourselves to look, with unblinking eyes, at exactly what happened, and to understand how the unthinkable, the unimaginable, ever happened. We are condemned to repeat history if we turn away, if we as a species allow ourselves to take the easy way out, to forget and let the lessons of the past fade away.

Dr. Fings was intrigued by my story. My own memories of the Holocaust, as well as my understanding of what happened to my parents and myself, were crucial to her ongoing research. It wrapped up a lot of loose ends for her, and I was more than happy to assist her document and comprehend what happened in Cologne, as well as what happened to the 2,011 Jews who were brought from Cologne to Łód.

We became friends over the phone and via email, as far as that is feasible. I respected her dedication to my family's story, which I had grown to believe was just mine. As it turned out, there were just two living survivors of the 2,011 Jews transported from Cologne to ód at the time.

At one point in our correspondence, Karola indicated that the NSDOK museum and the city of Cologne were planning an event to commemorate the seventieth anniversary of the deportations from Cologne to ód in the summer and fall of 2011.

She urged me to go to Cologne, Germany, for the occasion. She even suggested she could get the City of Cologne to invite Susan and me and cover our trip fees. She thought it would be significant and meaningful to have one of the two real survivors of the Cologne transports and the ód ghetto there to bear witness to what had happened and to help honor the memories of all those who never lived to tell the world about what they had gone through. She told me that only 23 of the 2,011 Jews abducted from Cologne by the Nazis survived the war. And, after all those years, I was the only one of those 23 who could attend the remembrance.

The prospect of returning to Germany worried me. Going back, with my teeth gritted, to the country that had dubbed me a virus and was bent to my annihilation felt like a terrible proposition.

But, in the spirit of telling my experience, which I had been doing at the Museum of Tolerance in Los Angeles once a month since 1977, I eventually decided to go. It was an emotional, profound, and life-changing experience. Susan, her sister, her brother-in-law, and I were greeted with a red carpet by Dr. Fings. She showed us around Cologne and even took us to view my parents' Stolpersteine, which stood in front of our old flat at 15 Blumenthal Strasse.

Of course, neither my mother nor father had a gravestone. They, like millions of their fellow Jews, were simply erased from the face of the earth by the Nazis. But now I knew where I could go to experience their spirits and be with them. I'm sure they'd be comforted to know that, while they—and practically the entire rest of our family—didn't survive the slaughter and terror, their son did. And knowing that, despite their perverted and cruel attempts, their tormentors are now almost all dead and gone. But here I am, still standing with them, still living and respecting their memories. We knocked on the door of our previous residence. An elderly woman glanced through the curtains, but she refused to approach the door. She was probably too afraid and unclear of who we were and what we wanted to let us into her life, even for a few minutes.

However, the couple on the next floor heard us and opened their door to welcome us in. They welcomed us inside their home, which was an exact replica of our previous one downstairs. They listened to our story and were astounded to learn about the old, cruel history of their apartment building, street, city, and people. They couldn't have been more accommodating.

As part of the seventieth anniversary celebration, Jürgen Roters, the Lord Mayor of Cologne, asked me to speak at the official reception to a room full of invited guests, including the US Consul General, several foreign diplomats, and some of Karola's colleagues from the NSDOK museum. Here's what I said in English, translated from my quaint 1930s-vintage German.

"Honored Lord Mayor Rotors and invited guests,

First, please forgive me for speaking in my old-fashioned German. It is the first time I have spoken it in almost seventy years, and this is the first time I have ever given a speech in my native language. I had vowed in 1945—for reasons you can probably understand—to never set foot on German soil again. Until this visit, I have kept that vow.

I am now breaking that vow. I am not making this journey out of mere curiosity. I am not here for a vacation. I am certainly not here for my own pleasure.

I am here to honor my parents and my sixteen other family members who were "resettled"—that is, taken away to die—in 1941. I am here to honor the 2,011 Jews of Cologne, of whom I am one of just two survivors, who in 1941 were sent from this place to the death, the disease and the starvation of the Litzmannstadt-Łódź ghetto.

After Łódź I survived Birkenau, Auschwitz and Buchenwald. My presence here today proves to the world that even now, after seventy long years, the total elimination of Jews from Cologne was not successful. The people who kidnapped and murdered my friends and family—nearly everybody I had ever known—are gone. But I am still here, speaking to you today.

When these horrible events took place, the world failed to understand how a seemingly civilized and cultured people could allow themselves to be so willingly and tragically misled. We try very hard, but we still fail to understand this today. And we can be sure that we will fail to understand it in the eternal future. We will never understand it. All we can be sure of is that we cannot forgive, and must never forget.

I chose to return to Cologne after these seventy years to assure the present generation of Germany that they need not carry the burden of guilt and shame of a generation past. The sins of the fathers, though unforgivable and incomprehensible to us today, should not be visited on their sons and their daughters.

Hate only begets hate. Tolerance should be the goal of the future, of all the human race. Tolerance should be the goal of the aggressors of the past. It should also be the goal of their victims.

In the name of my wife, my family and the other Litzmannstadt-Łódź survivors here with us today, I thank you, Lord Mayor, and the City of Cologne, for your kind invitation and hospitality."

The contents of this book may not be copied, reproduced or transmitted without the express written permission of the author or publisher. Under no circumstances will the publisher or author be responsible or liable for any damages, compensation or monetary loss arising from the information contained in this book, whether directly or indirectly. .

Disclaimer Notice:

Although the author and publisher have made every effort to ensure the accuracy and completeness of the content, they do not, however, make any representations or warranties as to the accuracy, completeness, or reliability of the content. , suitability or availability of the information, products, services or related graphics contained in the book for any purpose. Readers are solely responsible for their use of the information contained in this book

Every effort has been made to make this book possible. If any omission or error has occurred unintentionally, the author and publisher will be happy to acknowledge it in upcoming versions.

Copyright © 2023

All rights reserved.

Printed in Great Britain
by Amazon